Dedication

To my beautiful and brilliant wife, Eileen,
without whom none of this would be possible.

Special thanks to Alu Axelman, Bill Walsh, and
George Johnson for their review and input.

Table of Contents

6

In a time of deceit, telling the truth is a revolutionary act." -- George Orwell

In a world bound by chains,
A family struggles to remain.
A system that knows no bounds,
Their love and hope, it drowns.

Though a work of fiction, this story draws inspiration from surveillance technologies that pervade our world today. If left unchecked, the scenario painted within this first chapter could become a hauntingly accurate reflection of life in the not-so-distant future. This book aims to shed light on the truth behind the tale, unearthing the grand designs to bring such a reality into existence— even in places like the United States. More importantly, the bulk of this book seeks to equip you with the knowledge and tools necessary to combat this burgeoning tyranny. The time to act is now; the power to change the course of our future lies within our grasp.

Chapter 1: The Price of Submission

It took barely a decade for the world they knew to crumble. After a series of planned economic crises and the rise of authoritarian regimes, the world saw the widespread adoption of social credit systems and central bank digital currencies (CBDCs). By 2032, New York City, once bustling with life and energy, had been transformed into a dystopian nightmare. The United States, previously a symbol of freedom and democracy, had succumbed to digital tyranny. Despair and hopelessness filled the city, with the relentless onslaught of propaganda on the airwaves and the constant hum of drones overhead, casting dark, oppressive shadows on the streets below.

Surveillance had become a way of life, with security cameras on every street, face scanners in every building, and tracking built into every mobile device. The very idea of privacy had been erased, supplanted by the unrelenting gaze of the government, now capable of monitoring, controlling, and manipulating citizens' lives with chilling precision.

In this grim reality, the universal basic income concept (UBI) had been twisted into a means of subjugation. Although everyone received UBI, the amount depended on an individual's social credit score. High scores granted a comfortable lifestyle, while low scores condemned people to destitution. Society had devolved into a ruthless game of paranoia, compliance, and survival.

Healthcare access was strictly controlled, and people could be required to justify their presence or whereabouts at any time. Vaccine passports were not only mandatory but weaponized to control access to public spaces, transportation, and some jobs.

The social credit system ensnared entire families, with the scores of each member affecting every aspect of their lives. Those with low scores found themselves trapped in substandard housing, with limited transportation options and inadequate healthcare.

Amid the suffocating atmosphere of this dystopian society, the Johnson family struggled to maintain a semblance of normalcy. Jason and Kristin, college sweethearts who had once envisioned a bright future together, were now the doting parents of Wyatt, a curious and artistic teenager, and Emily, their fiercely determined and kind-hearted college-aged daughter.

They shared a modest pod in one of the numerous towering skyscrapers that defined the city's skyline, a stark reminder of the oppressive world they now inhabited.

Jason and Kristin bore the weight of knowing a time before the Bureau of Global Nations (BGN) centralized and controlled every aspect of life. They shared stories with Wyatt and Emily of a freer past, recounting cherished memories of family picnics in Central Park and laughter-filled movie nights, hoping to instill in their children the value of the liberties they had lost and the importance of striving for a better future.

The allocation of living spaces within these massive structures strictly adhered to the hierarchy imposed by social credit scores. As a result, the Johnsons, like countless others, lived in perpetual fear of the relentless surveillance that scrutinized their every move. They understood that any deviation from the BGN's stringent rules could upend their lives, threatening their home, access to education, and even their freedom.

Navigating this harrowing world, the Johnson family found solace in their love for one another. They clung to the hope that their bond would shield their children from the insidious forces, both human and systemic, seeking to rob them of their privacy, liberty, and dignity. Unbeknownst to them, a single careless act would set off a series of tragic events, threatening not only their already precarious standing within society but also the very fabric of their family's unity.

One evening, the family gathered in the cramped living quarters of their pod for their usual dinner ritual. Jason's face was drawn, and the tension in the room was palpable.

"Jason, is everything alright?" Kristin asked, noticing her husband's unusual behavior.

"I... I don't know. I shared an article on the CryptoForAll forum, criticizing the government's new more stringent restrictions and punishments for possessing illegal cryptocurrencies," Jason admitted, hesitating.

"You did what?!" Kristin gasped. "You know how dangerous that is! Even talking about it at home is dangerous. If anyone finds out, it could destroy our social credit scores!"

"I know," Jason said, his voice low. "But I couldn't stand by while they strip us of our last remaining freedoms. I had to do something."

Wyatt chimed in, "But Dad, it's not just about you. Your actions affect all of us. Now, we're all in danger."

"I understand, Wyatt," Jason said solemnly. "But I couldn't stay silent."

The weeks that followed were a downward spiral for the family. Emily, attending college, unwittingly used an incorrect pronoun when addressing one of her professors during a group discussion. The incident, caught on camera by the ever-present surveillance system, was immediately reported to the university's administration and to the government's Bureau.

The Bureau, zealous in enforcing its stringent regulations, imposed penalties on Emily and her family. As a result, their social credit scores plummeted even further, exacerbating their precarious situation. Emily was mandated to attend sensitivity training sessions and faced heightened scrutiny from her peers and faculty. The once-promising college experience she had hoped for turned into a suffocating environment where every interaction felt like walking on eggshells.

The final straw came when Kristin, in an attempt to make ends meet, sold some personal items on eBay to cover their basic needs. She managed to make $700 from the sales, which she hoped would help alleviate some of the family's financial burdens. However, Kristin failed to report the income to the government as required by the stringent financial regulations.

The government's ever-watchful eye, aided by powerful algorithms tracking financial transactions, flagged the discrepancy in Kristin's reporting. Within days, officials arrived at the Johnsons' doorstep, presenting them with a notice of violation. The family was hit with a devastating penalty – not only did they have to pay back the unreported amount but also faced a hefty fine, further plunging them into debt.

Their social credit scores took yet another hit, making it even harder for them to access essential services, find better housing, or secure loans. The incident also put Kristin's various jobs in jeopardy, as her employers became wary of associating with someone who had run afoul of the government's regulations.

In the aftermath of this crushing blow, the Johnson family felt the weight of the surveillance state more heavily than ever before. Their dreams of a better future seemed to crumble before their eyes, as they struggled to navigate the complex web of rules and regulations imposed by the omnipotent government Bureau.

"Jason, what are we going to do?" Kristin asked, tears streaming down her face. "Our social credit scores are so low, we'll lose everything."

"I... I don't know," Jason replied, his voice barely audible. "But we'll find a way. We have to."
The family huddled together, holding on to one another for support as they faced the grim reality of their situation. Little did they know, the worst was yet to come.

As the family's social credit scores continued to plummet, they faced increasingly severe consequences. They were no longer eligible for their pod's amenities, their access to high-speed transportation was restricted, their Wi-Fi slowed, their healthcare coverage was downgraded, and they faced public humiliation as their credit scores and reasons for their decline were shared throughout their community on social media.

One evening, Wyatt returned home from school, visibly upset. "Dad, some kids at school were bullying me today because of our low social credit scores. They called us "hoodlums" and said we don't deserve to live in the city. Even my friends avoid being around me because they don't want to be associated with someone who is blacklisted."

With deep empathy, Jason enveloped his son in a warm embrace and whispered, "I'm so sorry, Wyatt. People can be heartless, but we must never allow their venomous words to shape our identity or diminish our worth."

Meanwhile, Emily's college education was in jeopardy. Her scholarships were revoked due to the family's social credit score, and she was struggling to keep up with her studies while searching for a job to pay for college. Her degree at the university was fully paid for by a scholarship based on the family's high social credit score. The drastic collapse in the score left her responsible for the tuition or face expulsion within weeks.

"Dad, I don't know if I can continue going to college," Emily confessed one day. "I'm so far behind, and I can't afford tuition anymore. I've applied for several jobs that seemed promising but have met with nothing but rejection. One HR representative bluntly told me that they simply couldn't trust anyone with a social credit score as low as mine. I literally was scorned for having the audacity to even apply for the job . . . it turns out that if a company has even one employee with a credit score below 600, they are ineligible for any government contracts and must pay all sorts of extra fees and carry extra insurance."

"We'll find a way, Em," Jason reassured her. "We're not giving up."

As the pressure mounted, the family's relationships began to fracture. Jason and Kristin argued late into the night, their voices barely muffled by the thin walls of their new, smaller cramped pod. The once-happy family was slowly being torn apart by the unforgiving social credit system.

One day, Jason made a life-altering decision. "Kristin, I've been doing some research," he said, his voice trembling. "There's a program called MAID (Medical Assistance in Dying). It's... euthanasia. If I go through with it, your social credit scores will improve, and you and the kids will have a chance at a better life. It could take several years to get your scores higher, but with my score gone, you and the kids stand a chance. With my score, there is just no possible way to dig ourselves out."

"No, Jason, you can't!" Kristin sobbed, clutching her husband tightly. "There has to be another way. We'll find it, together." Jason replied flatly, "I went over the numbers with the public accountant at the town hall . . . my death would make you eligible for around $85,000 as a single mother of two children and will boost your social credit score by 100 points . . .that should help you dig out of this mess and get back on track . . . and if I let them give me some experimental medications to stop my heart, you will get even more money and an extra 50 points."

Jason had already made up his mind. "I love you, Kristin, but this is the only way I can see to save our family."

The family, heartbroken and defeated, gathered one last time before Jason's appointment with the MAID program. They held each other close, tears streaming down their faces, knowing that their lives would never be the same.

As Jason prepared to undergo the MAID program, his heart was heavy with the weight of his decision, but he knew that it was the only way he could save his family. He spent his final days with Kristin, Emily, and Wyatt, trying to create cherished memories that would sustain them in the difficult times to come.

On the day of the procedure, the family gathered in a sterile, cold room at the clinic, the walls painted with an impersonal shade of gray. Jason held Kristin's hand tightly, his eyes welling up with tears. "I love you," he whispered, as he tried to etch the image of her face into

16

his mind. Kristin sobbed uncontrollably, unable to imagine a life without her husband by her side.

Emily and Wyatt stood by their hearts aching and their minds unable to fully comprehend the gravity of the situation. They clung to each other for support, their tears streaming down their cheeks as they watched their father prepare to make the ultimate sacrifice.

As the medical staff began to administer the life-ending drugs, Jason's body tensed, his breathing labored. He looked at his family one last time, his eyes brimming with love, pride, and sorrow. The room was filled with the overwhelming sadness and grief of a family being torn apart by the cold, unfeeling grasp of the Bureau's CBDC and social credit system.

As Jason's heart slowed to a stop, Kristin, Emily, and Wyatt crumpled to the floor, their cries echoing through the empty halls of the clinic. In that moment, they truly understood the cost of living under the oppressive thumb of the Bureau – the price of their freedom, the life of a loving husband and father.

As the first glimmer of dawn broke through the darkness, Jason's sacrifice brought a flicker of hope to his family, their social credit scores rising like a phoenix from the ashes. Yet, emotional turmoil and a chain of heart-wrenching events shrouded this fleeting improvement, leaving Kristin, Emily, and Wyatt to traverse the labyrinth of their fractured lives, grappling with the void left by a beloved husband and father.

Bearing the weight of financial responsibility, Kristin balanced a plethora of jobs, exhaustion an ever-present specter. Moments, once cherished with her children, now evaporated like the morning dew. Still, her indomitable spirit shone through, leaving handwritten notes of love and encouragement for Emily and Wyatt each day.

"Stay strong, Em. Your father would be so proud," Kristin's note read one morning. Emily, burdened by the chasm her father's absence left and the relentless demands of her studies and new job, withdrew into a world of isolation. Her once-vibrant spirit, a tapestry of dreams and ambition, became ensnared in a void of emptiness. In rare moments, Emily found solace with her childhood friend, Jenna.

"Em, I know it's hard, but you can't let this break you," Jenna implored, her words a lifeline to Emily's drowning soul.

Wyatt's torment at school persisted despite the family's improved social credit scores. Relentless bullying drove him into the deceptive embrace of prescription painkillers, an addiction that spiraled into a whirlpool of despair. Neighbors' hushed whispers pierced the air, their once-welcoming smiles now frigid masks of indifference.

In a haze of intoxication, fate struck a cruel blow as Wyatt died in a tragic accident. The news spread like wildfire, further isolating the family within their tight-knit community.

As dark clouds gathered on the horizon, Emily confronted the debilitating side effects of a newly mandated vaccine. Despite the crippling consequences, she dutifully received her monthly boosters. A novel vaccine, designed to combat adult acne, unleashed a tempest of suffering within 48 hours of administration. Emily's health deteriorated with alarming speed, rendering her a prisoner within the claustrophobic confines of their 200-square-foot pod.

Their social credit scores, once ascendant, plummeted in response to Emily's collapsing GPA and Kristin's public denunciation of the vaccine. The family found themselves exiled to a smaller, suffocating pod—a constant reminder of the iron grip the government Bureau exerted over their lives.

Kristin's once-unyielding resolve began to tremble like a flickering flame. She found herself questioning the path she had chosen and the society that seemed bent on their destruction.

"Is this the world we fought so hard for, Jason?" Kristin whispered; her words lost in the shadows.

Still, she clung to hope, researching alternative treatments for Emily, and contacting advocacy groups for support. One evening, as Kristin sat with Emily in their dimly lit pod, she held her daughter's hand and whispered, "I'm so sorry, Em. I wish there was more I could do for you."

In that moment, a notification chimed on Kristin's phone—an email from a support group, offering guidance and resources to help them fight back against the oppressive system. With renewed determination, she decided they would not yield to despair.

"We will rise above this, Em. Together, we'll make a change," Kristin vowed, her voice a beacon of hope in the darkness.

Emily, her face pale and drawn, offered a weak smile. "Maybe you could find those herbs you told me about that helped grandpa when he got sick? I know that it is illegal to grow anything, but just maybe they can help me." Kristin hesitated "Em, I have already asked everyone I thought I could trust about getting them, but the Bureau is tightening the penalties, and no one wants to get involved."

"Mom, how did it ever get like this? How could people just let them take everything they had away? Your first home with a yard? Your freedom to travel to visit friends? I remember you telling me stories when I was a little girl about growing real strawberries and watermelon...." Emily's voice trailed as she drifted off, exhausted from the weight of it all.

Kristin lamented the past possibilities, broken dreams, and the stark future realities – "If only I could turn back time and have made the harder choices, we wouldn't be victims of this system."

In the throes of their struggle, the family grappled with the inescapable grip of the omnipotent Bureau, CBDC, and social credit system. Gazing into the vast, uncertain abyss of their future, they clung tenaciously to the merest whisper of hope—hope that, against all odds, a brighter tomorrow awaited them. In the darkest corners of their minds, the thought of MAID lingered as a haunting reminder of the lengths they might have to go to break free from their shackles.

The haunting tale woven within these pages, echoing the dystopian visions of Black Mirror and the literary masterpieces of George Orwell and Aldous Huxley, serves a dire purpose: to confront you with a stark choice between rising against the encroaching surveillance state for a brighter future or succumbing to the inescapable grip of tyranny. Every element of this narrative springs from today's unsettling realities, from China's social credit system to New York City's pronoun laws and Canada's MAID program. Governments are ceaselessly striving to mold a future where surveillance and centralized control reign supreme.

This is not a far-flung sci-fi fantasy; it is a looming possibility. This book aims to sound the alarm, educating you about the existing technologies and the political ambitions driving their implementation. Halting this relentless march demands awareness and decisive action. The time for complacency or the belief that "this could never happen in America" has long passed.

In the chapters that follow, you will discover that the technologies and systems discussed are not mere concepts but are already being trialed and adopted in the United States. At the heart of this dystopian nightmare lies the Central Bank Digital Currency (CBDC), which empowers governments to manipulate behavior through social credit scores, vaccine passports, and more by leveraging digital, programmable, and censorable money. Stopping CBDCs can thwart everything else.

The solution is clear, though not as simplistic as casting a vote. Members of Congress, who draw power from their monopolistic control of currency, are unlikely to vote for a reduction in their control or authority. The true power resides with the people.

By divesting from unstable fiat currencies (currencies backed by nothing but trust in the governments that issue them to repay their debts) and embracing self-custody cryptocurrency, gold, or silver, we can prevent the implementation of CBDCs and safeguard our liberties. In this book, we will show you how to do all of this and take control of your own financial freedom.

Time is of the essence; we have less than 12 months to act.

Artwork

"The only way to deal with an unfree world is to become so absolutely free that your very existence is an act of rebellion." - Albert Camus

In shadows they watch, the all-seeing eye,
Surveillance encroaches, as freedom waves goodbye.
From China's vast network to our homeland's reach,
Silent whispers of control, a lesson they teach.

CBDCs rise, as the social score looms,
Euthanasia programs, the end that consumes.
Yet, within this darkness, a spark ignites,
A call to resist, to defend our rights.

As we journey together through this chilling tale,
Let us not cower, let us not fail.
For the future's uncertain, but our resolve is clear,
We shall stand united and conquer our fear.

Chapter 2: Too Close for Comfort

In Chapter 1, we delved into a chilling dystopian future where personal freedoms were relentlessly controlled and monitored by an unforgiving system of rewards and punishments. As we venture into Chapter 2, we must face a disconcerting reality: many of the oppressive elements portrayed in our fictional narrative are already taking shape across the world.

This chapter will guide you through a thought-provoking exploration of the real-life systems and technologies that echo the haunting story of Chapter 1. We will examine the mechanisms that facilitate authoritarian control, such as social credit systems linked to Central Bank Digital Currencies (CBDCs), Universal Basic Income (UBI), vaccine passports, and even state-endorsed assisted death programs. Furthermore, we will delve into current-day punitive measures that closely resemble the chilling consequences from our dystopian tale, revealing the unsettling proximity between fiction and the world we inhabit.

Together, we will unravel the threads that bind our imagined dystopia to the emerging realities of our time, emphasizing the urgent need for awareness and action to safeguard our freedoms and resist the encroachment of tyranny.

The chapters ahead, unlike chapter 1, are not fiction.

Why This Chapter Matters

Grasping the implications of new technologies and governmental initiatives is fundamental to our ability to safeguard our liberties effectively. It is by scrutinizing real-world instances of surveillance systems, social credit scores, and vaccine passports, that we can assess the potential risks they present and adopt necessary countermeasures. This understanding equips us to make prudent decisions that maintain personal freedom and ward off the advances of oppressive control.

China: Social Credit Scores

In the preceding chapter, we bore witness to the harrowing descent of the Johnson family's social credit score, an unnerving plunge into an abyss where every action, every decision, was ruthlessly scrutinized and judged. Now, we stand on the precipice of a chilling reality - this dystopian nightmare is not confined to the realm of fiction. Social credit systems are not only existent, but they are also proliferating.

China stands at the forefront, operating the most expansive social credit system in the world. However, it's not an isolated case. Countries like Singapore, South Korea, and the United Arab Emirates have also adopted similar systems, albeit on a smaller scale. Even the United States, with its financial credit score system, teeters on the edge of a slippery slope. A few calculated tweaks by the Federal Reserve and the government could thrust the nation into a full-fledged system akin to China's.

Let's pause for a moment and picture the harsh reality of living under the weight of a social credit system. Your every move is under scrutiny, your every decision, noted. Your value as a citizen is reduced to a mere number, constantly fluctuating based on your conformity to societal norms and regulations de jour. This dystopian vision is the everyday reality for the people of China, where the social credit system was launched with great fanfare in 2014. The stated aim? To build a "trustworthy" society by regulating individual and corporate behavior.

The system operates like an omnipresent digital specter, ceaselessly collecting and analyzing data from an array of sources - government records, financial transactions, even your social media activity. It all feeds into an algorithm that assigns a dynamic numerical score to each individual and business. This score, reflecting your so-called 'trustworthiness,' wields the power to determine your access to fundamental rights and opportunities, such as housing, education, travel, banking, and employment.

Consider the case of Zhejiang Province, where the social credit system reveals its teeth in full measure. Here, citizens are categorized into credit tiers based on their scores, as illustrated in Table 1:

Score Range	Credit Tier	Description of Benefits
850-1000	Excellent	Individuals with high social credit scores may enjoy benefits such as easier access to loans, better interest rates, preferential treatment in various services, and more.
700-849	Good	Individuals with good scores usually have access to most public services and face fewer restrictions than those with lower scores.
550-699	Fair	Individuals in this range might face some restrictions or challenges when accessing certain public services or applying for loans.
300-549	Poor	Individuals with low social credit scores may face significant restrictions, such as limited access to loans, travel, and certain public services.
0-299	Very Poor	Individuals in this range may experience severe penalties and restrictions on their daily lives, including limited access to public services, travel, and financial products.

Table 2 offers a peek into the detailed mechanics of the social credit system, outlining how specific actions may potentially influence a citizen's social credit score. Keep in mind that these figures are approximations:

Activity	Points Change
Volunteering in community service	15
Charitable donation	10
Paying bills on time	5
Failing to properly sort and recycle waste	-5
Smoking in a non-smoking area	-10

Cheating in a video game	-15
Running a red light	-20
Defaulting on a loan	-30
Spreading false information online	-50
Fraudulent use of government subsidies	-100

An alarmingly large percent of Chinese citizens find themselves trapped in the lowest credit echelon, constantly battling a barrage of restrictions and penalties due to their diminished scores.

Let's take a sobering dive into the life of Chinese journalist Liu Hu, who found himself ensnared in the thorny grasp of the social credit system after daring to challenge the government's actions. Known for his fearless investigative journalism on government corruption, Liu attracted the state's ire, resulting in a crushing drop in his social credit score. The ramifications were swift and severe: barred from acquiring property, denied loans, and restricted from purchasing high-speed train tickets, Liu's life was turned upside down.

The oppressive nature of the social credit system hasn't escaped the notice of international observers. Maya Wang, a stalwart researcher at Human Rights Watch, condemns the system as a "potent tool for social control" that can be wielded to suppress dissent, activism, or criticism of the government. Similarly, Samantha Hoffman, a fellow at the Australian Strategic Policy Institute, cautions us about the emergence of a "culture of surveillance, fear, and control," where citizens live in constant apprehension of how their every action might affect their score.

China's social credit system stands as a chilling testament to the potential for governmental control and surveillance to infringe upon individual freedoms. The realities faced by citizens in Zhejiang Province and the sobering experience of Liu Hu serve as stark illustrations of the ethical dilemmas and potential dangers of such an all-encompassing surveillance apparatus.

Central Bank Digital Currency (CBDC)

The Johnson family's social credit score was inseparably tethered to their digital currency, morphing into an insidious tool for the government to deny them access to services based on their compliance (or lack thereof) with state directives. As we will delve into in Chapter 4, every major industrial nation on the globe is currently in the throes of developing their own Central Bank Digital Currency (CBDC), with China blazing the trail through their Digital Currency Electronic Payment (DCEP).

Initiated back in 2014, the development of the DCEP has been a slow burn, with pilot projects springing up in cities across China since 2020. Now, the project has expanded, collaborating with banks, tech behemoths, and payment platforms to usher in the era of the CBDC for the masses. An array of heavy hitters, including the People's Bank of China, Tencent, Alibaba, and JD.com, are at the heart of the DCEP's development and implementation. Guided by the iron hand of the Chinese Communist Party (CCP), the DCEP is poised to morph into a ubiquitously adopted and centralized form of digital currency.

Among the most worrisome facets of China's DCEP is the potential for it to merge with the nation's social credit system. This amalgamation would gift the government with unprecedented control over its citizens, allowing it to keep tabs on and manipulate their financial transactions. The fusion of the CBDC and social credit scores paints a dystopian picture of an all-seeing surveillance state, where financial behavior directly impacts social standing and access to services. Imagine a world where your financial transactions hinge on your social credit score: your attempt to purchase meat is declined due to your carbon credits being maxed out for the month; you're denied a high-speed train ticket because your score is too low; your children are barred from participating in extracurricular activities because of your vocal opposition to a school rule - these are just a few of the terrifying potential scenarios.

Leading experts have expressed profound concerns about this system's impact on individual freedom and privacy. Martin Chorzempa, a research fellow at the Peterson Institute for International Economics, warns that "China's CBDC, coupled with the social credit system, could concoct the perfect storm for an unparalleled level of control over citizens' lives, enabling the government to monitor and steer financial behavior to an alarming extent."

In a similar vein, Eswar Prasad, a professor of trade policy at Cornell University, comments that "the unholy alliance of CBDC and the social credit system raises the specter of a surveillance state that could curb individual freedoms and suppress dissent, radically redefining the dynamic between the state and its citizens."

Universal Basic Income (UBI)

In Chapter 1, we were front-row spectators of the government's manipulation of the Johnson family. Their primary tool of control? Adjusting the volume of Central Bank Digital Currency (CBDC) funneled to the family each month in the form of a Universal Basic Income (UBI). CBDC, digital currency conjured up by central banks and governments, and UBI, a policy dictating the quantity of CBDC dispersed to citizens, have the potential to amplify the level of state control over the populace.

UBI is an age-old concept, captivating minds for centuries and put forth by thought leaders such as Thomas More and Thomas Paine. More's *Utopia* painted a picture of a society where basic necessities were provided for by the government, irrespective of one's work status. Paine's "Agrarian Justice" posited a world where every person enjoyed a "basic income." Today, this concept is experiencing a revival, with pilot programs dotted around the globe probing its practicality.

UBI enthusiasts trumpet its potential to abolish poverty, shrink income inequality, and provide a buffer against the job losses expected with advancing automation and Artificial Intelligence (AI). Detractors argue it could inflate government spending, sap work incentives, and stoke inflation. Further, economists like Robert Murphy caution that UBI might breed a dependency culture, with citizens leaning on government handouts instead of their own hard work. Conversely, tech mogul Elon Musk has argued that with robots encroaching on human jobs, UBI might become an inevitability.

Finland's UBI experiment in 2017-2018, which granted €560 per month to 2,000 unemployed individuals, yielded ambiguous results. While participants reported improved well-being and reduced stress, the effect on employment rates was negligible. Critics like Olli Kangas, the study's leader, argued that the pilot's design was inherently flawed, making it impossible to draw definitive conclusions about UBI's viability. Authors like Alu Axelman point out that socialist policies are far more likely to have substantially better outcomes when implemented in small, homogenous places like Finland.

In the US, UBI rode the wave of Andrew Yang's 2020 presidential campaign, with his proposed $1,000 monthly "Freedom Dividend." Despite Yang's unsuccessful bid for the Democratic nomination, UBI's flame has remained lit, with localized programs sprouting across the nation.

The UBI debate is at a fever pitch considering the imminent AI revolution and anticipated job losses due to skyrocketing productivity and efficiency. Still, it isn't a stretch to envisage a dystopian reality where UBI morphs into a tool for complete population control. Tying UBI payments to compliance with government rules could usher in an era of pervasive surveillance and control. As Dr. Karen Kornbluh, a senior fellow at the German Marshall Fund, warns, "Without adequate checks and balances, UBI could become a tool to manipulate citizens' behavior, making dissent and noncompliance expensive." MIT's Professor David Autor adds that UBI, "if improperly designed, could morph into a social engineering tool, rewarding conformity and stifling dissent."

The US government's history of encroaching on its citizens' liberties, be it through the Patriot Act, Operation Chokepoint, or the proposed RESTRICT Act (which could allow unprecedented control to the President and Secretary of Commerce, potentially stifling free speech and criminalizing the use of VPNs to access foreign websites, among many other dystopian elements within the bill), is a chilling reminder. Even if UBI comes with 'proper safeguards,' one can't ignore the likelihood of another 'emergency' conveniently eroding those safeguards. Remember COVID?

Vaccine Passports

The COVID-19 pandemic and ensuing government response have underscored the emergence of vaccine passports, both globally and within the United States. These passports, digital or physical documents that validate an individual's COVID-19 vaccination status or test results, have become a hotbed of controversy and division. They serve as a ticket to travel, attend events, or enter certain venues, thereby acting as evidence of undergoing a specific medical procedure required to participate in those activities.

Numerous programs have seen the light of day around the world, such as the European Union's Digital COVID Certificate, Israel's Green Pass, the United Kingdom's NHS COVID Pass, and the Excelsior Pass in New York State. While their requirements and breadth vary, they share a common goal — compliance with government regulations and meticulous monitoring of citizen behavior.

Civil liberties champion Silkie Carlo warns, "Vaccine passports infringe upon personal freedom and privacy. They risk engendering a divided society where the unvaccinated are pushed to the fringes." Bruce Schneier, a cybersecurity expert, raises concerns about the possible intertwining of vaccine passports and social credit scores, cautioning, "If vaccine passports become gatekeepers to essential services, it's conceivable they could merge with social credit systems, thus diluting individual freedoms and bolstering state control."

The fusion of vaccine passports with Central Bank Digital Currencies (CBDCs) and social credit scores could potentially amplify existing apprehensions. By binding financial transactions and creditworthiness to vaccination status, governments could exercise an unparalleled degree of control over their citizens. In the hands of an oppressive regime, this could pose grave threats to societal well-being. For example, in Australia, parents who don't adhere to the prescribed vaccination schedule face the denial of numerous welfare payments. Bioethicist Arthur Caplan cautions, "In the absence of vigilance, the amalgamation of CBDCs, social credit scores, and vaccine passports could forge a system where individuals are pressured into compliance, thereby eroding the bedrock of democratic societies." Remember that the same people who wanted to round up the unvaccinated are the same people who want to take away personal defense tools.

As we continue wrestling with the COVID-19 pandemic, mounting evidence suggests that the vaccines may not be as "safe and effective" as initially claimed. It's now clear that millions of Americans were leveraged into taking a medical procedure under misconceptions, misrepresentation, and lacking genuine informed consent. Vaccine mandates and the consequent rise of vaccine passports pose a tangible threat to personal freedom and privacy. With hundreds of vaccines in the pipeline, including those employing the mRNA technology featured in most COVID-19 vaccines, the list of federally mandated vaccines for children is swelling, jumping from five in 1970 to over 17 in 2021 and growing.

Canada: MAID Program

As depicted in Chapter 1, to improve his family's social credit score and thus their life prospects, Jason made the heart-wrenching decision to end his life via the MAID program. Surely, this must be a work of fiction? However, a glance at Canada reveals that state-endorsed euthanasia is a troubling and expanding reality. Since its establishment in 2016, Canada's Medical Assistance in Dying (MAID) program, originally designed to alleviate the suffering of terminally ill patients and offer them dignity, has evolved into a multifaceted and contentious issue with worldwide ramifications.

Detractors of the Canadian MAID program worry that it might set a precarious precedent with potentially hazardous outcomes. Dr. Susan McDonald, a specialist in palliative care, voices her concern: "The expansion of the MAID program could lead to a societal acceptance of euthanasia, possibly exposing vulnerable individuals to coercion or misuse."

The possible convergence of the MAID program with social credit scores and Central Bank Digital Currencies (CBDCs) sketches an even darker landscape. Imagine a society where a person's social credit score sinks too low, and assisted suicide is presented as their sole option. Under the dominion of a tyrannical government, this could be leveraged as an instrument for population control and coercion.

Such a grim possibility evokes the dystopian 1976 film *Logan's Run*, wherein assisted suicide is institutionalized as government policy. In this movie, a dystopian society manages population levels by mandating the extermination of all citizens upon reaching the age of 30. The parallels between Logan's Run and the potential misuse of the MAID program are striking and serve as a cautionary tale.

While the MAID program's official aims center on offering a compassionate option for those facing unbearable suffering, we're aware that governments tend to expand their authority, often leading to unforeseen repercussions. The potential merger with social credit scores and CBDCs raises deep-seated ethical questions. This program could metamorphose into a mechanism for oppressive governments to exert dominance over their citizens, coercing them into compliance. Canada's euthanized 10,000 citizens in 2022 and its announced plans to extend the program to people with mental disabilities shows that the slope can indeed be perilously slippery.

The Surveillance State

In Chapter 1, the Johnson family's every move was meticulously tracked, a scenario eerily reminiscent of today's China. China's surveillance state stands unrivaled in its expanse and intricacy. The country's burgeoning surveillance infrastructure encompasses an impressive array of technologies, from CCTV cameras and facial recognition software to biometric monitoring and AI capabilities. This intricate surveillance network, designed to maintain control over its populace, has emerged as a global concern.

China is estimated to host over 200 million security cameras, a number that continues to rise annually. This omnipresent surveillance ensures that citizens are perpetually monitored in public spaces, making anonymity virtually extinct. Additionally, China's national ID system, which obligates citizens to supply a spectrum of personal information, including biometrics, further cements the government's hold over its people. AI is leveraged to analyze the mind-boggling volume of data amassed, enabling the authorities to preempt and quell potential threats to the regime. With the recent passage of e-verify in the US, there will be an ushering in of biometrics and personal information tied to employment mirroring the Chinese system.

China's surveillance efforts have been particularly oppressive towards the Uighur Muslim minority, subjecting them to invasive monitoring and stringent restrictions on their freedoms. Advanced facial recognition technology is deployed to track and control the Uighur population, leading to widespread human rights violations.

A complicated network of private companies supply surveillance services and technology to the Chinese government. These firms, including Huawei, ZTE, and TikTok, have been accused of providing equipment and services that facilitate spying on other nations. Moreover, China has gained notoriety for its cyber espionage activities, with state-sponsored hackers targeting foreign governments and corporations to pilfer sensitive data.

The scale of data collection in China is astounding, with facts revealing:
- The creation of billions of data points daily by China's surveillance network.
- The government's aim is to construct a comprehensive database that encompasses all its 1.4 billion citizens.
- Data collection that delves into personal details like religious beliefs, political affiliations, and daily routines.

- The use of AI technology to process and analyze this massive amount of data, allowing authorities to track and predict citizens' behavior.

China's surveillance state continues its rapid expansion, with plans to install hundreds of millions of additional cameras in the coming years. Sophie Richardson, China Director at Human Rights Watch, observes, "The Chinese government's use of surveillance technology is so pervasive and intrusive that it's changing the very nature of what it means to be a citizen in China." Maya Wang, Senior China Researcher at Human Rights Watch, adds, "China's surveillance state is creating a new kind of totalitarianism that is unprecedented in human history."

However, mass surveillance isn't limited to China; nations worldwide, including the US, have been implementing comprehensive surveillance systems. Edward Snowden's revelations about the National Security Agency's (NSA) surveillance activities revealed the extent of the US surveillance state and sparked major concerns about individual privacy and government overreach. Some of Snowden's top 10 revelations about the US surveillance state encompass:

- NSA's data collection on domestic and international phone calls and internet communications.
- The PRISM program, granting NSA access to data from major tech companies like Google, Apple, and Facebook.
- The XKeyscore program allows NSA to sift through vast amounts of internet data.
- The tapping of undersea fiber-optic cables to intercept global communications.
- The tracking of cell phone locations worldwide.

- The hacking of foreign governments and corporations.
- The weakening of encryption standards.
- Warrantless wiretapping of American citizens.
- The use of facial recognition technology.
- The sharing of surveillance data with foreign governments.

The growth of surveillance in the US is also evident through the increasing number of security cameras and the collection of data. Some startling statistics include:

- An estimated 85 million security cameras are in use in the US.
- The number of security cameras in the US is estimated to grow to 125 million by 2025.
- On average, Americans are captured on camera around 75 times per day, and that's not just counting selfies.

If you assumed that the US Government curtailed its surveillance of US citizens after Snowden's revelations, you might want to reconsider that assumption. The explosive "Twitter Files," leaked in December 2022, uncovered a chilling reality: Twitter had been clandestinely cooperating with the US government to surveil its citizens on a large scale. These alarming documents reveal that Twitter has been providing sensitive user data to the government, including names, emails, phone numbers, and IP addresses, as well as access to search and content moderation algorithms.

The revelations extend even further. Twitter, along with Facebook, Google, and other tech giants, and the US government (including NSA, FBI, CIA, DHS, and DOD), have been conspiring to devise new methods of tracking and censoring non-conforming information and alternative views of citizens on their platforms. This breach of privacy highlights that big tech is not just a neutral platform for free speech; it has been used as a tool for government surveillance and the suppression of dissent.

The Twitter Files expose the staggering extent of government surveillance and manipulation of the narrative and raises urgent questions about the invasion of citizens' privacy and access to personal, private information. With the government's unrestricted access to vast quantities of personal data, awareness and protection of your privacy have never been more critical.

The COVID-19 pandemic spurred further expansion of the surveillance state, with measures like contact tracing (also involving the big tech giants) being implemented to purportedly curb the virus's spread. These measures have raised concerns about the potential for long-term government tracking of citizens.

In Chicago, for example, the city has deployed thousands of security cameras integrated with advanced facial recognition technology. This development has sparked debates about privacy and the balance between public safety and civil liberties. Snowden's statement about government surveillance rings true: "Arguing that you don't care about the right to privacy because you have nothing to hide is no different than saying you don't care about free speech because you have nothing to say."

We've shed light on the alarming reality that the dystopian programs depicted in Chapter One are not mere fiction but have parallels in today's world. Prepare to be taken aback as we delve into how the very behaviors penalized in Chapter One are already attracting retribution from various governments in 2023.

From facing penalties for sharing content on social media to the chilling reality of state-sponsored euthanasia, the line between fiction and reality is becoming increasingly blurred. The future we once feared is unfolding before our very eyes, making it crucial to acknowledge these developments and act before it's too late.

When Memes Lead to Misdemeanors: The Guilty Verdict in the Douglass Mackey Case

In a situation mirroring Chapter One of Jason Johnson's narrative, where the lead character faced penalties for circulating content about decentralized cryptocurrencies, a pro-Trump internet troll named Douglass Mackey has been convicted for attempting to deceive voters into not casting their ballots for Hillary Clinton in the 2016 presidential election through misleading memes. Operating under the Twitter pseudonym "Ricky Vaughn," Mackey disseminated images that mimicked counterfeit Clinton advertisements, implying that individuals could vote via text rather than in person.

Mackey's legal representatives maintained that he was merely sharing light-hearted memes, while the prosecution contended that his actions deliberately targeted black voters and women. The American Civil Liberties Union (ACLU) spoke out harshly against the verdict, "The conviction of Douglass Mackey for posting memes is a dangerous precedent that threatens free speech. Memes are a form of political expression, and the government should not be in the business of prosecuting people for expressing their political views, even if those views are unpopular. This conviction sets a dangerous precedent that could be used to silence dissent and stifle free speech in the future." Mackey could face up to a decade in jail and a fine amounting to $250,000 for his conviction. His sentencing is scheduled for August 15, 2023.

Weaponizing the Internal Revenue Service (IRS)

In a bold and audacious step, the government is set to bolster its IRS forces with a staggering addition of 87,000 armed IRS agents. House Speaker Kevin McCarthy articulates, "The IRS is on a recruitment drive to enlist an army of 87,000 armed agents, with the aim to conduct more audits on Americans like you. That's a force larger than the entire populace of Joe Biden's hometown of Scranton, PA." While the official target is touted to be the ultra-rich, historical evidence suggests that it's the poor and middle-class citizens who often end up bearing the burden of these audits. Indeed, a ProPublica report indicates that Americans benefiting from the Earned Income Tax Credit (EITC) face audits at a higher frequency than all but the wealthiest taxpayers, despite being among the least affluent households.

Drawing parallels to Kristin's situation in Chapter One, who suffered penalties for not declaring an eBay transaction, the IRS has recently issued a warning to Americans to report payments exceeding $600 received through platforms such as Venmo and PayPal. This policy shift has sparked an uproar among citizens, who perceive it as a flagrant violation of privacy and a stark overextension of government power. It is expected that these new IRS agents will be more likely to scrutinize your garage sale transactions or gig work rather than focusing on those capable of hiring high-priced attorneys to counteract.

Envision a world where every transaction, regardless of its size or importance, is under the vigilant scrutiny of government operatives. The freedom to conduct business and manage your personal finances, once deemed an intrinsic right, now rests in the hands of an increasingly intrusive bureaucracy.

He Said, She Said, They Fine: The Pronoun Police Strike Again!

Drawing parallels to another scenario from Chapter One, Emily encountered repercussions for the incorrect use of a pronoun. This echoes the stringent pronoun usage regulations in New York City, where a misstep in identifying a person's chosen gender can result in penalties as steep as $250,000. The gravity of this punishment has ignited fervent debate and resistance, particularly from those who argue that such rules infringe upon the fundamental rights to freedom of speech and expression.

Unforced Error: Djokovic Denied Entry to Miami Open Due to Vaccine Passport

The vaccine passport from Chapter One finds a real-life counterpart in the case of Novak Djokovic, the tennis superstar who was denied entry to the Miami Open due to his unvaccinated status. This event has ignited a heated debate about the fairness and potential overreach of vaccine passport mandates, with critics arguing that they infringe on personal liberties. Kevin Mitchell from the Guardian further explained, "Djokovic's case has also had a significant impact on the tennis world. He is one of the most popular and successful players in the history of the sport, and his absence from major tournaments has been a major blow to the sport. It remains to be seen how Djokovic's vaccination status will affect his career in the long term. However, it is clear that this is a major issue that is likely to continue to be debated for years to come."

Death for Disability: The Dystopian Reality of Canada's Military Veteran Support System

Finally, the dystopian MAID (Medical Assistance in Dying) program from Chapter One echoes chillingly in the real-life story of Christine Gauthier. This Canadian Paralympian and veteran was shockingly offered the Canadian government's aid to end her life when all she requested was a wheelchair lift for her home. Recalling her interaction with the VA during her testimony before the House of Commons, Gauthier stated, "I have a letter saying that if you're so desperate, madam, we can offer you MAID, medical assistance in dying."

It isn't a significant leap from Gauthier's experience to that of the Johnson family in our not-too-far-off narrative set in 2032. Canada has even expanded this program to include individuals with mental disabilities and those of a younger age. A 25-year-old man from British Columbia, Canada, was offered the MAID program after expressing suicidal thoughts stemming from his inability to find a romantic partner. The unidentified man, while on a crisis hotline, voiced his feelings of hopelessness and isolation. He expressed his long-standing, unsuccessful attempts at finding a girlfriend, coupled with his battles with depression and anxiety.

The objective of this chapter is to ring the warning bell: the technological framework for a global control system is not only established but is undergoing testing worldwide. The stark reality is that governments are either planning or already implementing programs designed to monitor, control, and manipulate the behavior of their citizens through digital currencies and a pervasive surveillance infrastructure. The dystopian future from Chapter 1 is unfurling, and our window to act is dwindling, measured in months rather than years. Our collective action is needed to stop the spread of Central Bank Digital Currencies, the foundation upon which all the other oppressive systems will anchor. As we will explore in the last half of the book, moving out of the dollar and into self-custody crypto, gold, and silver is the best path for stopping CBDC.

This chapter has uncovered the existence of technology for mass control and surveillance and highlighted governments' readiness to micromanage and penalize their citizens for seemingly innocuous actions.

As we move into the next chapter, we'll delve into the driving forces behind this worldwide push towards centralization. Far from being random, we will examine the Non-Government Organizations (NGOs) that have been working for decades to establish a global government and centralized system for managing human behavior.

As we journey ahead, prepare yourself for an in-depth exploration into the philosophical underpinnings of CBDCs – a globalist movement driven by centralization, determinism, and fear. By understanding the motivations and ideologies fueling these systems, we'll be better equipped to oppose and ultimately dismantle them. Together, let's strive to create a future where financial freedom and individual autonomy aren't merely safeguarded but are indeed celebrated.

6 Key Takeaways from Chapter 2:

- The foreboding world painted in Chapter One isn't merely a work of fiction, but finds unsettling parallels in our reality, such as the Canadian MAID program and China's surveillance apparatus.

- The potential for misuse of programs like euthanasia can engender grave ethical quandaries and could potentially pave a perilous path towards population control.

- China's sprawling surveillance network bears significant implications for personal privacy and human rights, particularly for marginalized communities like the Uighurs.

- The creeping prevalence of surveillance systems in nations such as the United States sparks critical debates about privacy, civil liberties, and the potential for government overreach.

- Cases of individuals facing penalties for online content, financial transactions, or pronoun usage demonstrate the intensifying influence of technology on personal freedoms.

- A viable strategy to counteract the surge of CBDCs may involve destabilizing the banking system through withdrawing fiat currency and embracing alternative financial tools like self-custody cryptocurrencies, gold, and silver.

Artwork:

"I think one of the biggest existential risks is that we will end up with a one-world government, and I don't think that's a good thing. I think it's important to have diversity of thought and diversity of governance. I think it's important to have different countries with different cultures and different ways of doing things. I think that's what makes the world interesting." – Elon Musk

In shadows cast by giants tall,
The central banks conspire,
With power, money, influence,
Their grip on us grows tighter.

Together now, they forge a chain,
Of digital control,
CBDCs the link they seek,
To bind each heart and soul.

Resist we must, this creeping tide,
Of centralization's wrath,
For freedom's call still echoes strong,
And guides us on our path.

Chapter 3: The Centralization Agenda: CBDCs and the Power Grab of International Organizations

As we venture further into the complex landscape of CBDCs, it's time to uncover the real intentions driving the worldwide rush to adopt them. CBDCs are often portrayed in mainstream discourse as the inevitable evolution of money, promising to enhance financial inclusion and combat illicit activities. Yet, as we move through this chapter, you'll find George Orwell's words echoing in your mind: "Political language... is designed to make lies sound truthful and murder respectable, and to give an appearance of solidity to pure wind."

In this part of our journey, we pull back the curtain to reveal the clandestine globalist agenda fueling the CBDC movement—a concerted effort among influential figures in business, government, and technology to amass power, wealth, and information. These individuals often work through international bodies such as the United Nations (UN), World Economic Forum (WEF), World Bank, International Monetary Fund (IMF), and Bank of International Settlements (BIS), all of which have long championed a centralized, one-world government framework. The advent of CBDCs offers them an expedited path to achieving this goal.

Imagine a world where centralization grapples with decentralization, fear contends with hope, and determinism battles free will. The globalist agenda seeks to centralize power under a technocratic elite, utilizing fear as a weapon to advance their plans. This struggle, in essence, is a contest between light and dark, freedom and control.

In this chapter, we'll scrutinize five key organizations that are propelling this centralized, fear-centric agenda:

- The UN - which aims to centralize political authority.
- The WEF - striving to concentrate business control in the hands of a select few multinational corporations.
- The World Bank - wielding financial power to shape economic development in emerging nations.
- The IMF- enforcing global economic policy compliance.

- The BIS - masterminding the operations of central banks, thereby manipulating the world's financial system.

We'll delve into the history, evolution, and involvement of these organizations with CBDCs, as well as their interconnectedness. However, a word of caution: once the veil of illusion is lifted, there's no going back. The rabbit hole of truth is deep, and what lies beneath can be unsettling. Prepare yourself for a revelatory journey through the labyrinth of global power, as we shine a light on the reality lurking behind the façade.

Why This Chapter Matters

Understanding the globalist momentum behind CBDCs and their centralization objectives is crucial in formulating effective countermeasures. By laying bare the orchestrated actions of entities like the UN, WEF, IMF, World Bank, and BIS in their quest to centralize power through CBDCs, we illuminate the challenges they pose to individual freedoms. This insight empowers us to resist initiatives that diminish personal autonomy and gravitate towards alternatives fostering decentralization.

Highlighting the technocratic and elitist motivations steering the centralization agenda sparks the discernment and determination essential for standing against it. In this rapidly evolving financial landscape, our commitment to preserving personal liberties and championing decentralized solutions is paramount.

The Rise of Fear-Based Centralization

The term "technocracy" was coined by the Californian engineer, William H. Smith, defining it as "the governance of the populace made operative through their intermediaries, the scientists and engineers." This term was later employed to depict Thorstein Veblen's works, endorsing the notion of elitists appointing scientists and engineers to administer society in a top-down manner. The technocracy movement picked up momentum until its abrupt halt in 1933. To witness technocracy in action, a revisit of Aldous Huxley's dystopian masterpiece, Brave New World, suffices. In the contemporary reading of this novel, one discerns the absence of a political system, devoid of voting or the notion of individual rights.

In Huxley's narrative, the World State governs the entire planet. The World State epitomizes technocracy as it's directed by technocrats—individuals possessing specialized knowledge in science and technology, superseding elected representatives. These technocrats navigate society through the mastery of biology and psychology, exercising control over the social fabric, resource distribution, and even citizens' emotions and cognitions. Conventional constructs of family, emotional bonds, and personal independence are forsaken for the benefit of societal stability and efficiency.

Through his novel, Huxley criticizes a technocratic system pushed to its furthest boundaries, illustrating a society where technical specialists reign supreme, yet individual freedom and identity are drastically compromised. It reveals the potential dehumanization that could transpire if technocratic ideologies are not counterbalanced with concerns of human rights, personal liberty, and moral and ethical restrictions.

Huxley's brother, Julian Huxley, who was himself a technocrat, eugenicist, a proponent of a unified world government, and the founding director of UNESCO

(United Nations Educational, Scientific, and Cultural Organization) will be discussed later. This piece of information is crucial in comprehending the operations of the aforementioned five organizations.

While the technocracy movement paused in 1933, it rapidly revived in 1973 with the establishment of the Trilateral Commission by David Rockefeller and Zbigniew Brzezinski (who later became National Security Advisor to President Jimmy Carter and father to MSNBC news host Mika Brzezinski). Brzezinski and Rockefeller were fervent supporters of technocracy and the progression towards a unified world government. The Trilateral Commission aimed to drive a unified direction for Europe, North America, and the Asia Pacific.

One of the significant accomplishments of the Trilateral Commission was to conceptualize what was later adopted by the UN in 1974 as the New International Economic Order (NIEO). The NIEO has evolved into a crucial component of the UN 2030 Sustainable Development Goals, the foundation for a unified world government and a top-down technocratic system of governance and control.

While the UN is the primary public entity advocating for the global unification of power and control, the actual propulsion towards centralization stems from nebulous groups operating behind the scenes that guide and manipulate a concealed agenda. Organizations like the Trilateral Commission, Bilderberg Group, Council on Foreign Relations, and The Club of Rome clandestinely orchestrate a global strategy, the funding and implementation of which are undertaken by large international organizations financed by taxpayers or colossal, multinational corporations.

The sociological concept of organized incompetence is occasionally leveraged by the elite to retain control or propel a concealed agenda within hierarchical structures. This tactic frequently hinges on the compartmentalization of information and power, where each hierarchical level has less access to information than the level above, creating an effective veil over the broader picture and preventing lower-level individuals from grasping the full situation or the true motives of the elite. Furthermore, stringent certification requirements can cultivate a culture that prioritizes strict conformity to established protocols and procedures, often discouraging questioning or challenging the status quo. Employees are encouraged to concentrate on their specified tasks without comprehending or questioning the wider implications. The outcome can be an institution where many individuals unknowingly facilitate the advancement of hidden agendas. This tactic leverages the human inclination to evade uncertainty and pursue stability, making it a subtly potent tool for those at the hierarchy's pinnacle to consolidate power and control.

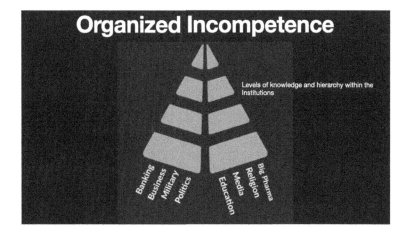

Before we delve into the intricate details of each of the five global powerhouses pushing a one world government technocracy, let's take a moment to consider the sheer magnitude and influence of these entities and their roles in the realm of CBDCs. By the end of this chapter, it's likely you'll be convinced that there's an orchestrated strategy at play, aiming to centralize currency and manipulate human behavior through synchronized policies across these groups.

The following table offers a comparative snapshot of the World Economic Forum (WEF), United Nations (UN), International Monetary Fund (IMF), World Bank, and Bank for International Settlements (BIS). It provides a high-level overview of their respective budgets, employee counts, and specific roles in relation to Central Bank Digital Currencies (CBDCs). It's important to note that the figures for budgets and employee numbers are approximate, subject to change as the organizations evolve and adapt.

Organization	Budget (approx.)	Number of Employees (approx.)	Roles with respect to CBDCs
UN	$5.4 billion (2023)	44,000 - excluding 'peacekeepers'	- Encourages discussion and cooperation on CBDCs and digital currencies - Supports research and policy development related to digital finance
WEF	$528 million (2023)	800	- Promotes dialogue and collaboration on CBDCs and digital currencies - Facilitates research and discussion on CBDCs and financial innovation
World Bank	$13.6 billion (2023)	10,000	- Supports research and dialogue on CBDCs and digital financial inclusion - Assists countries in the development and implementation of digital finance strategies
IMF	$14.5 billion (2023)	2,900	- Conducts research and analysis on CBDCs and their potential impact on the global economy - Provides guidance and recommendations for countries considering CBDC implementation
BIS	$1.1 billion (2023)	2700	- Research CBDCs and their implications for monetary policy and financial stability - Collaborates with central banks on CBDC development and implementation

Each of these organizations has a unique part to play in the ongoing conversation and cultivation of CBDCs. Their involvement spans a broad spectrum, from conducting in-depth research and analysis to proffering policy recommendations and providing technical support. While their main mandates and areas of concentration may diverge, they are united in their common goal: driving the progression and centralization of CBDCs.

The United Nations (UN) - A Wolf in Sheep's Clothing

The United Nations, born out of the ashes of World War II with a mission to foster peace and international collaboration, harbors a hidden side that often lies concealed beneath the cloak of its ostensibly humanitarian endeavors. To the discerning observer, the UN emerges as a critical puppeteer in the globalist theatre, weaving narratives of fear, centralization, and determinism in its quest for global governance.

The UN's journey began in 1945 as a phoenix rising from the failed League of Nations. Its initial lofty aims of promoting peace, championing human rights, and driving economic development have gradually morphed into a broader ambition: the centralization and control of the most critical aspects of the lives of the global population.

H.G. Wells, the famous author who played a part in the inception of the League of Nations and publicly advocated for the UN's creation, once wrote, "Countless people...will hate the New World Order...and will die protesting against it." This so-called New World Order is gradually taking shape through the UN's Agenda 2030, an expansive plan encapsulating 17 Sustainable Development Goals (SDGs). While these goals might seem benign or even admirable on the surface, a deeper inspection reveals a blueprint for concentrated control:

Development Goals (Agenda 2030)	Control and Reduced Freedom Aspects
1. No Poverty	Centralizing control over poverty alleviation efforts, potentially reducing individual choice and self-reliance
2. Zero Hunger	Centralizing global food security initiatives, potentially limiting local food production autonomy and choices
3. Good Health and Well-being	Centralizing healthcare policies and systems, potentially restricting individual healthcare choices
4. Quality Education	Centralizing education systems and standards, potentially limiting diverse educational approaches and choices while promoting indoctrination
5. Gender Equality	Centralizing gender policies and initiatives, potentially undermining cultural diversity, and traditional values
6. Clean Water and Sanitation	Centralizing water and sanitation management, potentially reducing local control and resource autonomy
7. Affordable and Clean Energy	Centralizing energy policies and infrastructure, potentially limiting individual and community energy choices
8. Decent Work and Economic Growth	Centralizing economic and labor policies, potentially restricting individual employment and entrepreneurial opportunities
9. Industry, Innovation, and Infrastructure	Centralizing industrial and infrastructure development, potentially reducing individual innovation and local autonomy
10. Reduced	Centralizing efforts to reduce

Development Goals (Agenda 2030)	Control and Reduced Freedom Aspects
Inequalities	inequalities, potentially limiting individual freedoms in pursuit of equality (think equality of outcome not equality of opportunity)
11. Sustainable Cities and Communities	Centralizing urban planning and development, potentially reducing local decision-making and individual property rights
12. Responsible Consumption and Production	Centralizing resource management and production, potentially limiting consumer choices and local production autonomy
13. Climate Action	Centralizing climate policies and initiatives, potentially restricting individual, and local environmental choices
14. Life Below Water	Centralizing ocean and marine resource management, potentially limiting local and individual marine resource usage
15. Life on Land	Centralizing terrestrial ecosystem management, potentially restricting individual land use and local autonomy
16. Peace, Justice, and Strong Institutions	Centralizing governance and justice systems, potentially reducing individual freedoms and local self-governance
17. Partnerships for the Goals	Centralizing global cooperation and partnerships, potentially undermining national sovereignty, and individual freedoms

From its post-World War II origins as a peacekeeping body, the UN's mission has incrementally expanded, morphing into a global architect influencing the lives and liberties of every person on earth. For some key players, however, this was always the destination — the establishment of a one-world government. Julian Huxley, the inaugural Director-General of UNESCO (a UN agency) and sibling of Aldous Huxley, the author of the dystopian masterpiece, *Brave New World*, once said, "Political unification in some sort of world government will be required." It's clear that the groundwork for Agenda 2030 has been laid over decades.

As the UN's membership has swelled to include virtually all nations, its power and influence have grown in tandem. The body now molds global policy across a spectrum of areas, from economics and climate to human rights. And now, it's stepping into the realm of CBDCs. Secretary-General António Guterres highlighted how CBDCs could turbocharge the sustainable development goals mentioned earlier: "Digital finance technologies can be game changers for the financing of the Sustainable Development Goals." We can swiftly connect the dots here — in the UN's perspective, digital finance (CBDCs) could be a mechanism to enforce Agenda 2030 and ensure compliance in areas from healthcare to food security to climate change. For instance, your social credit score and access to CBDCs could be tied to your carbon footprint. What does that look like? You could be denied use of air travel, purchasing meat, or access to services because you have already used up your carbon credits for the month.

The blueprints are being crafted globally, with pilot programs being launched within individual nations. In the same way that U.S. states are often referred to as independent laboratories for policy, different countries are testing grounds for these strategies, all with the end goal of launching a single, unified, global system. It seems we are on the precipice of a very real "Brave New World."

Expect the UN to employ fear tactics when introducing these programs. Let's take a moment to revisit how the UN has leveraged fear and hysteria in the past:

Year	Controversial Statement from UN
2005	"The United States is responsible for most of the world's problems."
2007	"The internet should be regulated to prevent hate speech and extremism."
2009	"Climate change is the greatest threat to humanity."
2011	"Capitalism is a major cause of poverty and inequality in the world."
2012	"The United States should pay reparations for slavery."

The World Economic Forum (WEF)

The World Economic Forum (WEF), since its inception in 1971 by Klaus Schwab, has evolved from a modest consortium of European business leaders into a powerful hub for global centralization, increasingly skewing the scales in favor of the world's elite. Nestled in the murky depths of global power networks, the WEF has been shaping the trajectory of big business, with its annual Davos summit serving as a high-profile platform for this mission.

The WEF's advocacy consistently tilts towards the advantage of big business, often at the detriment of

60

small businesses and entrepreneurial endeavors. Here are a few illustrative examples:

- Exclusive Membership: The WEF predominantly draws its membership from large multinational corporations, leaving small businesses out in the cold.
- Annual Meetings: The Davos summit primarily invites top executives, world leaders, and influential figures, creating a power vortex in favor of big business.
- Public-Private Partnerships: Endorsing such partnerships often leaves small businesses struggling in the shadows of their larger counterparts.
- Regulatory Influence: The WEF's policy-shaping influence frequently results in regulations that cater to the whims of big corporations, posing barriers for smaller competitors.
- Access to Global Leaders: The WEF provides big businesses with a direct line to political leaders, creating a platform for lobbying and influence-peddling that often undermines the interests of the world's citizens.
- Networking Opportunities: Events like Davos offer the elite a chance to build powerful alliances, often to the detriment of smaller competitors.
- Thought Leadership: The WEF's reports and guidelines often revolve around the interests of big businesses.
- Globalization: The WEF's push for globalization has bolstered large corporations while stifling opportunities for small businesses.
- Sustainability Initiatives: The WEF's focus on sustainability often results in policies that disadvantage small businesses due to high

compliance costs, while paving the way for big corporations to flourish.

The WEF's commitment to centralization and its alignment with the interests of multinational corporations paint a clear picture of its elitist, technocratic nature. As The Daily Telegraph aptly stated in January 2021, "Klaus Schwab's world view is an undemocratic, technocratic, authoritarian one, where the world is divided between the elite who run things and the rest who are managed and manipulated by the elite for their own good." Canadian author and activist Naomi Klein adds, "Davos is the ultimate expression of the neoliberal order – a world of extreme corporate influence and extreme concentration of wealth."

The WEF's influence has permeated politics, with prominent politicians including Bill Clinton, Joe Biden, Donald Trump, and Tulsi Gabbard from the US, Tony Blair from the UK, Emmanuel Macron from France, and Justin Trudeau from Canada participating in their programs and/or speaking at their events. Over time, the WEF has experienced exponential growth in member companies, budget, employees, and influence, further solidifying its centralizing agenda.

The WEF's robust endorsement of CBDCs offers a stark testament to their unwavering commitment to centralization and elite control.
Here are some key facets of their engagement with CBDCs:
- Partnership with Central Banks: The WEF collaborates closely with central banks to investigate and shape the evolution of CBDCs.
- CBDC Policy-Maker Toolkit: The WEF has fashioned a comprehensive toolkit to assist

policymakers in the design and deployment of CBDCs.

- Research: The WEF consistently publishes research on the prospective benefits and challenges of CBDCs, typically leaning towards their implementation.
- Pilot Projects: The WEF lends its support and counsel to CBDC pilot projects.
- Carbon Footprint Tracking: The organization has proposed using CBDCs as an instrument to monitor individuals' carbon footprints, thereby bolstering their drive for centralization and control.

The WEF has been repeatedly criticized for leveraging fear and uncertainty to further its global agenda. By employing hyperbolic language and prophesying catastrophic outcomes, the WEF has successfully seized global attention and incited a palpable sense of urgency surrounding its contentious "Great Reset" initiative. This ambitious plan seeks to radically transform key sectors like energy, economy, healthcare, and education through the lens of technology and centralization, in alignment with the UN's Agenda 2030.

Critics contend that the WEF strategically capitalizes on public fear, creating an image of a world teetering on the brink, to champion their radical restructuring of existing economic and societal systems. Klaus Schwab, the founder and executive chairman of the WEF, epitomizes this approach with his statement: "The pandemic represents a rare but narrow window of opportunity to reflect, reimagine, and reset our world." Such pronouncements are often viewed as attempts to exploit the global crisis to further the WEF's agenda, rather than proposing authentic solutions for the betterment of humanity.

The World Bank

In the wake of World War II, the World Bank emerged as a beacon of hope, endowed with a noble mission to rebuild a world fractured by war. However, as times have changed, this beacon has morphed into a puppeteer, orchestrating the strings of centralized control.

The World Bank's inaugural project in 1947 was indeed admirable: granting a loan of $250 million to France for post-war reconstruction. Fast-forward to the early 2000s, the World Bank introduced a contentious program in Argentina with the intent to restructure its economy amid a harsh financial crisis. This initiative, known as the "Argentine Structural Adjustment Program," entailed sweeping privatization, deregulation, and fiscal austerity measures, as dictated by the World Bank and the IMF. This "shock therapy" approach resulted in widespread unemployment, poverty, and social turmoil, leaving the nation in an even more precarious state.

To capture the human cost of such policies, consider the story of Rosa, a 45-year-old widow and mother of two from a small Argentinian town. Prior to the crisis, Rosa had stable employment in a textile factory, ensuring a steady income for her family. However, the factory shut down as a direct consequence of the World Bank's policies, leaving Rosa unemployed. With scant savings and no government assistance, Rosa and her children were dislodged from their home and compelled to live in a makeshift shelter on the town's fringes.

As Rosa grappled with an increasingly deteriorating economy and job market, she was forced to scavenge for food in garbage dumps to feed her children. Her youngest child, Diego, aged eight, contracted a severe skin infection due to their unsanitary living conditions. However, he was unable to receive adequate medical treatment as public health services had been dismantled under the World Bank's policies.

The World Bank's invasive intervention in Argentina's economic affairs starkly illustrates its overbearing, centralized approach that infringes on national sovereignty. The late Argentine President Néstor Kirchner lambasted the World Bank's role in the crisis, stating, "The adjustment policies of the IMF and the World Bank brought about more hunger, poverty, and marginalization in our country. They made a few people richer at the expense of many who became poorer." Rosa's story is but one example of the catastrophic consequences when global financial institutions impose their agendas on sovereign nations and the profound personal impact on individuals like Rosa and her family.

Many scholarly works have delved into the damage inflicted by the World Bank across the globe. Here, we provide a high-level overview of just four categories of World Bank policies that underscore their severe tactics:

- Structural Adjustment Policies (SAPs): Forced indebted countries to adopt austerity measures, deregulation, and privatization. "The IMF and World Bank are like undertakers at a funeral. They come in when the economy is dead, and they take away the body." - Joseph Stiglitz, Nobel Laureate in Economics.
- Land Grabs: Encouraged foreign investment in agricultural land, leading to displacement of local communities. "The World Bank is facilitating land grabs and sowing poverty by putting the interests of foreign investors before those of

locals." - Anuradha Mittal, Executive Director of the Oakland Institute.

- Environmental Degradation: Funded projects that have caused deforestation, pollution, and loss of biodiversity. "The World Bank is fueling climate change, while pretending to fight it." - Tom Goldtooth, Executive Director of the Indigenous Environmental Network.

- Privatization of Water: Pushed for privatization of water resources, making it inaccessible to millions. "Water privatization under the guidance of the World Bank has been a massive failure and a violation of the human right to water." - Maude Barlow, Chair of the Council of Canadians.

The World Bank has grown into a behemoth, with more member banks, a larger budget, an ever-expanding workforce, and increasing influence on a global scale.

Now, the Bank has set its sights on Central Bank Digital Currencies (CBDCs). Here are three concrete examples:

- Nigeria: The World Bank worked with the Central Bank of Nigeria to develop the eNaira, centralizing financial power in the country.

- Framework Development: The World Bank partnered with the IMF to create a framework for CBDCs, potentially enabling a global digital currency system.

- Research and Guidance: The Bank has published numerous reports on the benefits and challenges of CBDCs, shaping global policy on digital currencies.

In a chapter 4, we'll thoroughly examine the Nigeria case study, focusing on its eNaira project and how the World Bank's involvement has influenced its development.

Like the UN, the World Bank has faced allegations of utilizing fear tactics to extend its sway over financial and economic policies in developing countries. By raising the specter of looming debt crises and economic disasters, the organization coerces these nations into accepting its loans and adopting its suggested structural reforms. The World Bank capitalizes on the precarious state of struggling economies, taking advantage of their anxieties about financial collapse to impose policies that frequently benefit Western interests. Joseph Stiglitz, former Chief Economist at the World Bank, illuminates this issue: "In the World Bank's programs, the real aim often seems to be not development, but rather ensuring the interests of Western financial markets." This comment underscores the concerns that the World Bank's fear-driven strategy may ultimately further its own agenda, rather than genuinely catering to the needs of the countries it professes to assist.

The International Monetary Fund (IMF)

Emerging from the devastation left by World War II, the IMF was initially established to help rebuild and stabilize the world's shattered economies. However, as time progressed, the IMF's mission transformed from a benevolent force of reconstruction into a shadowy puppet master orchestrating a globalist agenda of centralization and control.

In 1947, the IMF's first project involved providing financial aid to post-war France to restore its economy and stabilize the exchange rate. At the time, the IMF's actions were considered helpful and necessary, but it was unknown that the foundations of global control were already being laid.

The IMF's infamous intervention in Greece during the Eurozone crisis in the 2010s serves as a prime example of its invasive approach that infringed upon a nation's sovereignty. As part of the "Troika" (IMF, European Central Bank, and European Commission), the IMF imposed severe austerity measures on Greece, demanding drastic spending cuts, tax increases, and structural reforms in return for bailout funds. These policies resulted in widespread social and economic chaos, with soaring unemployment rates, deteriorating public services, and countless individuals pushed into poverty.

One poignant example of the devastating effects of the IMF's program is the story of Nikos, a 50-year-old father of three from Athens. Before the crisis, Nikos owned a small, prosperous family restaurant passed down through generations. However, as austerity measures took effect, his business suffered from higher taxes, reduced public spending, and a dwindling customer base. Ultimately, Nikos was forced to close his restaurant, leaving his family without income.

Unable to find work, Nikos and his family faced eviction from their home and struggled to provide food. His children, once optimistic students, now dealt with the psychological trauma of their family's collapse. His teenage daughter, Eleni, had to abandon her dream of attending university due to the family's financial situation and the soaring cost of education under the IMF's policies.

Former Greek Finance Minister Yanis Varoufakis criticized the IMF's approach, stating, "The IMF's program for Greece had a disastrous effect on our social fabric, pushing our people into abject misery." Nikos' story serves as a stark reminder of the human cost of the IMF's forceful interventions, highlighting the tragic consequences that can result when an external financial institution disregards a nation's sovereignty and the welfare of its citizens.

Recently, the IMF provided a bailout to Argentina (which, despite the bailout, is still experiencing 100% MONTHLY inflation) on the explicit condition that Argentina does not make Bitcoin legal tender. In essence, the IMF seeks monopoly control and will use its power to stifle competition.

As with the World Bank, numerous books have been written about the effects of IMF overreach. For the interest of brevity, I will showcase five high level categories of IMF egregious behavior:

- Austerity measures: The IMF's insistence on austerity measures has had disastrous effects on countries like Greece, plunging them further into debt and economic turmoil.
- Structural adjustment programs: These programs force developing countries to adopt policies that prioritize the interests of foreign investors over their own citizens.
- Currency devaluation: The IMF's push for currency devaluation can lead to rampant inflation and economic instability.
- Bailout conditions: The IMF's bailout conditions often involve controversial policies, such as deregulation and privatization, which can exacerbate existing problems.
- Crisis prevention: The IMF uses the fear of economic collapse to justify its intervention,

creating a self-fulfilling prophecy of crisis and control.

Over the years, the IMF has experienced significant growth in its number of member banks, budget, staff, and influence. From its origins as an organization with 29 member countries, the IMF now boasts a staggering membership of 190 nations, exercising unparalleled power over the global economy.

Is a Global Currency in the Pipeline?

The IMF has played a pivotal role in shaping the global monetary system. Through its history of engagement in worldwide financial initiatives, the IMF has been making strides towards a more unified currency system.

In 1969, the IMF introduced Special Drawing Rights (SDRs), a form of international monetary reserve asset. SDRs can be viewed as a sort of "money" invented by the IMF to assist nations in financial distress. You can think of SDRs as a universal gift card that countries can exchange to support each other during financial difficulties. This "gift card" can be converted into actual currency, thus facilitating international cooperation, and promoting global economic stability. Economist Richard Duncan underscores the significance of SDRs, asserting, "The Special Drawing Right may well become the global currency of the future. Given their past actions in 'assisting' financially troubled countries, it is conceivable that this could pave the way to tyranny."

CBDCs could escalate this power further. In April 2023, the Digital Currency Monetary Authority (DCMA) announced the Universal Monetary Unit (UMU), or "Unicoin," a significant step in global currency development. Revealed at an IMF meeting, the unveiling of the Unicoin underscores the IMF's role in shaping global currency trends. As an international CBDC, the Unicoin is designed to operate alongside national currencies, potentially guiding the world towards a unified global currency.

The IMF has also developed a CBDC handbook to support central banks and governments worldwide in their digital currency ventures. As per the "IMF Approach to Central Bank Digital Currency Capacity Development" report, the IMF's multi-year strategy for aiding CBDC rollouts includes the creation of a living "CBDC Handbook" for monetary authorities to consult.

Noam Chomsky, renowned linguist and political activist, has sounded the alarm about the potential consequences of further centralization and control by the IMF. He warns, "A global currency controlled by the IMF would give the IMF even more power than it currently possesses. This would be a dangerous development, as it would provide the IMF with the authority to dictate economic policy to countries worldwide."

Much like the UN and WEF, the IMF has often been accused of using fear tactics to encourage nations to implement austerity measures and economic reforms that align with the organization's agenda. The IMF capitalizes on moments of crisis and vulnerability, heightening economic anxieties, and promoting a narrative of impending disaster to justify its interventions. By doing so, the IMF pressures nations into accepting its financial assistance and implementing its proposed policies, even if they may not serve the best interests of the affected populations. Yanis Varoufakis, the former Greek Finance Minister, encapsulates this sentiment: "The IMF's powerful technocrats... have the capacity to induce a sense of panic, and then present their policies as the only antidote to this panic." This assertion implies that the IMF might use fear to wield control and propagate its policies, rather than offering authentic solutions tailored to the distinct needs and situations of each country it purports to assist.

The Bank of International Settlements (BIS)

Tucked away in the intricate fabric of the global financial system, the Bank of International Settlements (BIS) has served as the central bank for other central banks since its establishment in 1930. Emerging from the aftermath of World War I to manage Germany's reparation payments—a factor that contributed to Germany's severe economic hardship and led to World War II—the BIS has evolved into a formidable institution advocating for the centralization of money and banking. It's an entity renowned for its preference for large banks over smaller ones, and its intricate, often consequential, policies.

Take the Basel Accords, for instance, a set of regulations aimed at ensuring that banks maintain sufficient capital reserves. While the initial goal was to bolster the financial system, they favored larger banks, which have the resources to maneuver through intricate regulations. Conversely, smaller banks grapple to keep pace. This skewed landscape mirrors a Monopoly game where big banks begin with extra hotels, while small banks merely aspire to pass Go.

Moreover, the BIS's response to the 2007-2009 financial crisis involved infusing massive funds into the system, primarily benefiting large banks. The BIS justified this action as a requisite to prevent the entire financial system's collapse, once again employing fear tactics. However, this move perpetuated the "too-big-to-fail" mindset, leaving smaller banks marginalized and disadvantaged. As we scrutinize the implications of the latest Basel III regulations considering recent bank failures, including Silicon Valley Bank, Credit Suisse, First Republic among others, it becomes increasingly evident that the BIS's strategies are often excessively intricate, costly, and ineffective, exacerbating the obstacles faced by smaller financial institutions.

Over the years, the BIS has seen substantial growth in terms of member banks, budget, staff, and influence. Presently, it includes 63-member central banks, representing countries that account for approximately 95% of global GDP. Its influence has broadened, with the organization now hosting various committees that shape international financial regulations.

The BIS is also actively participating in discussions concerning both decentralized crypto and CBDCs. The BIS perceives decentralized cryptocurrencies like Bitcoin as a direct challenge to the authority and control of central banks. Hervé Hannoun, former Deputy General Manager of the BIS, emphasizes the importance of central banks retaining control, stating, "Central banks must retain their ability to control liquidity." Hyun Song Shin, Economic Counsellor and Director of the Monetary and Economic Department of the BIS, goes a step further, asserting, "Cryptocurrencies are a threat to financial stability and could undermine the role of central banks."

To counter the threat posed by decentralized cryptocurrencies, the BIS has been actively engaged in the research, development, and implementation of CBDCs. The BIS is invested in understanding the effects of CBDCs on financial stability, monetary policy, and cross-border payments.

The Great CBDC Convergence: How Major Institutions are Steering the Digital Currency Agenda

In the global theatre, the UN, WEF, IMF, World Bank, and the BIS are significant players, jointly fueling the momentum of the UN Agenda 2030.

The WEF, operating as a non-governmental entity, assembles leaders from diverse sectors to deliberate on worldwide issues. They are zealous advocates of the UN Agenda 2030, championing its cause through a series of events and initiatives.

Concurrently, the IMF, renowned for providing monetary aid to economically challenged nations, has pledged to assist these countries in achieving the UN Agenda 2030 goals. Tailored lending programs to meet these ends have been devised.

In parallel, the World Bank, another global entity offering loans and grants to developing countries, has vowed to support the UN Agenda 2030, with its lending programs engineered to align with these objectives.

Simultaneously, the BIS, a hub for global central bank cooperation, has pledged to aid nations in their pursuit of the UN Agenda 2030, pioneering various research and policy initiatives to further this ambition.

Collectively, these organizations—the UN, WEF, IMF, World Bank, and BIS—wield significant influence on the global economic stage. Through their endorsement of the UN Agenda 2030, they strive to ensure all nations implement it. Here's how they are contributing:

1. The WEF has initiated several programs to bolster 'sustainable development', such as the Global Shapers Community and the Young Global Leaders program.
2. The IMF has fashioned lending programs like the Resilience and Sustainability Trust Fund to assist countries in UN Agenda 2030 implementation.
3. The World Bank's efforts include lending programs like the International Development Association (IDA) for supporting nations in their quest to meet the UN Agenda 2030 goals.
4. The BIS has introduced initiatives like the Sustainable Finance Initiative to assist countries in achieving the UN Agenda 2030 goals.

In this context, these organizations have aggressively advocated for CBDC adoption, creating toolkits, guidelines, and policy briefs to advance their centralization-focused agenda.

Their shared themes include fortifying central bank control over the financial system, advocating for a standardized regulatory framework, and enhancing the security and efficiency of cross-border payments. They've been engaged in intensive dialogues on CBDCs, with central bankers, policymakers, and experts sharing centralization perspectives.

This collaboration also extends to research and policy initiatives, with bodies like the BIS Innovation Hub conducting CBDC explorations with input from IMF and World Bank expertise.

Understanding the history, intentions, growth, and collaboration of these groups over decades makes the idea of a global government, interlinked with megacorporations and controlling all aspects of human life via a global CBDC and social credit score, very plausible.

We now recognize that CBDC technology has been successfully deployed in countries like China and that influential global entities like the UN, WEF, IMF, World Bank, and BIS have clear intentions regarding the centralization of power, information, and money—with CBDCs being a primary vehicle for their efforts.

In the following chapter, we delve into the rapid global CBDC rollout. Major first world nations, including the United States, are developing or testing CBDCs. The controlled demolition of fiat currency is a fear-inducing plan, designed to make CBDCs acceptable. This can be countered by moving out of fiat and into self-custody crypto, gold, and silver. Decentralization, free will, and love have the power to quell the rising tide.

Key Takeaways from Chapter 3:

- Prominent entities such as the UN, WEF, IMF, World Bank, and BIS are striving to centralize authority via CBDCs, posing a significant threat to individual liberties. Their expansive resources and global clout make them formidable opponents.
- These organizations have championed centralized control for years, with programs like the UN's Agenda 2030 serving as conduits to extend their sway further.
- Their policy initiatives predominantly endorse centralization and top-down command, often compromising individual freedom and self-governance. Decentralized alternatives are noticeably absent.

- The CBDCs under development could bestow governments with unprecedented control over their citizens' financial affairs and behaviors. Rigorous oversight and protective measures are required to deter misuse.

- Upholding the principle of separating money and state is crucial to impede the spread of CBDCs and protect individual sovereignty. Financial self-reliance curbs governmental control.

- CBDCs are swiftly advancing across the globe, with over 100 countries at various stages of development. The peril of centralized control through digital currencies is rapidly evolving into a worldwide reality.

- Alertness, firm action, and alternative solutions are necessary to counter the centralizing tendencies of these influential institutions and safeguard fundamental freedoms. Shared awareness and grassroots mobilization might be our most effective defenses.

- Transitioning from fiat currency to self-custodied alternatives like cryptocurrencies, precious metals, and tangible assets can decelerate the advance of CBDCs, safeguard privacy and independence, and encourage financial sovereignty.

Artwork:

"We know that no one ever seizes power with the intention of relinquishing it."
- George Orwell, 1984

In the age of digital gold,
A tale of control and power unfolds.
From China to Nigeria, the US in sight,
CBDCs emerge, to rule and to smite.

Freedom and privacy, values we hold dear,
Vanish in silence, as the digital dollar draws near.
Resistance is needed, the time is now,
To fight for our rights and make a solemn vow.

For money and state should never entwine,
As we strive for a future, where freedom may shine.
Embrace self-custody, let crypto take flight,
Together we stand in this perilous fight.

Chapter 4: Digital Chains Unleashed: The Global Race Towards CBDCs and the Erosion of Freedom

In the previous chapter, we unveiled the chilling ambitions of powerful globalist organizations such as the UN, WEF, World Bank, IMF, and BIS, who are pushing for centralization and control through the implementation of CBDCs. Now, prepare to embark on a riveting journey as we delve into the rapid and alarming progress of CBDC research, development, and deployment worldwide. With gripping case studies from China and Nigeria, we'll explore the dark shadows of oppression and tyranny that loom over us as CBDCs become a reality. Brace yourself for the startling truth about expedited CBDC development in the US, including three successful pilot programs and the imminent rollout of FedNow in July 2023 - the very infrastructure that will pave the way for a CBDC. Time is of the essence, and our window to prevent a descent into global tyranny is rapidly closing.

Why This Chapter Matters

It is crucial to recognize the swift advancement of CBDCs globally, and the potentially dystopian future they might bring about, to motivate immediate actions to avert such scenarios. Examining instances of CBDC implementation in countries like China and Nigeria reveal the hazards of complete surveillance, manipulation, and privacy erosion. Bringing to light the US government's aggressive efforts to develop CBDCs necessitates a cautious and skeptical approach to its motives.

This awareness engenders a vital urgency to safeguard financial independence, autonomy, and individual sovereignty by swiftly transitioning to self-custody alternatives. It is essential to keep in mind that the opportunity to preserve our freedoms rests in our hands, and that the time to act is now, before it becomes a much steeper uphill battle.

The Global CBDC Landscape

As the grip of CBDCs tightens around the globe, we must face the reality that our financial future is becoming increasingly centralized and controlled. A staggering 114 countries, which represent over 95 percent of global GDP, are exploring CBDCs. In May 2020, merely 35 countries were considering a CBDC. Now, an alarming 60 countries have reached an advanced stage of exploration—either in development, pilot, or launch phases.

To date, 11 countries have fully launched a digital currency. China's pilot project has already reached 261 million people (representing 18.2% of the population) and is set to expand across most of the country by the end of 2023. Jamaica is the latest entrant to the CBDC race, launching the JAM-DEX. As these currencies spread like wildfire, it's clear that the world is shifting rapidly towards a digital financial future, where our everyday freedoms and privacy could rapidly become a distant memory.

The year 2023 is shaping up to be a pivotal moment in the advancement of CBDCs, with over 20 countries slated to take significant steps toward piloting a CBDC. Australia, Thailand, Brazil, India, South Korea, and Russia are all planning to continue or commence pilot testing in 2023. The European Central Bank (ECB) is also expected to start a pilot project next year.

As of December 2022, all G7 economies have entered the development stage of a CBDC. The US has completed 3 CBDC pilot programs (more details below) and is rolling out the infrastructure to make CBDC possible in July 2023! The US has transformed from research project into actual development, signaling the nation's commitment to embracing a centralized digital currency. This shift is only the beginning, as 18 of the G20 countries are now in the advanced stage of CBDC development. Of those, seven countries are already in the pilot stage, with nearly every G20 country having invested new resources in these projects and made significant progress over the past six months.

The rapid advancement of CBDCs raises concerns about the erosion of financial freedom and privacy. With central banks taking on a greater role in controlling the flow of money, we're witnessing a global push towards a dystopian financial landscape, where every transaction is monitored, and our economic lives are dictated by centralized authorities. The allure of CBDCs for governments is clear: they offer the ability to track and control money flows with unprecedented precision, while also enabling the seamless implementation of monetary and fiscal policies.

The accelerated timeline of CBDC implementation worldwide hints at a carefully orchestrated plan to consolidate financial power and control. Are we prepared to sacrifice our financial freedom and privacy for the sake of convenience and alleged innovation? This table provides a partial list of what we stand to lose if CBDC is fully deployed.

Potential Risks	Negative consequences
Total financial surveillance	Loss of privacy and anonymity in financial transactions, potentially leading to abuse of power by authorities.
Centralization of power	Central banks and governments could exert excessive control over citizens' financial lives.
Potential for censorship	Authorities could block or freeze transactions of certain individuals or groups.
Loss of financial autonomy	Individuals may become overly reliant on the central authority for their financial well-being.
Programmable money restrictions	Central authorities could impose specific conditions on the usage of funds, limiting personal freedom.
Negative interest rates	Central banks could impose negative interest rates directly on individuals' accounts, eroding

Potential Risks	Negative consequences
	savings.
Exclusion of vulnerable groups	Those without access to technology or digital literacy could be left behind, exacerbating inequality.
Cybersecurity risks	A centralized digital currency system could be targeted by hackers, leading to significant financial losses.
Systemic failures	Centralized digital currency systems may be vulnerable to technical glitches, causing widespread disruption.
Elimination of physical cash	The loss of physical cash may lead to a reduction in personal freedom and an increased reliance on technology.

Issues and Concerns Surrounding China's Digital Yuan

The digital yuan, China's ambitious foray into the realm of digital currency, has a concerning history rooted in the early 2010s, when the Chinese Communist Party (CCP) recognized the potential of cryptocurrencies to disrupt the global financial landscape. While initially emerging as a response to cryptocurrencies like Bitcoin, the digital yuan soon became a strategic tool for the CCP to tighten its grip on the economy and exert greater control over its citizens' financial lives.

Unlike decentralized cryptocurrencies, the digital yuan operates within a centralized framework controlled by the People's Bank of China (PBOC), ensuring the government's authority over its use remains unchallenged. This centralization raises alarming questions about privacy and surveillance, as the digital currency enables the CCP to monitor and track every transaction, reinforcing its stronghold on the nation.

The digital yuan, also known as Digital Currency Electronic Payment (DCEP), functions through a two-tier system designed to maintain the government's control. In the first tier, the PBOC issues the digital currency to commercial banks, while in the second tier, these banks distribute it to the public. Users access the digital yuan through digital wallets, allowing the government to monitor and regulate transactions and payments with unprecedented precision. While the CCP claims to offer "controllable anonymity," the reality is that anonymity is far from absolute. True privacy with the digital yuan is as elusive as an invisibility cloak with a neon sign proclaiming, "I'm invisible!" As Yaya Fanusie, a former CIA analyst, aptly puts it, the digital yuan is about "the CCP having control over the financial system at the next level."

The CCP's unwavering commitment to the digital yuan is evident in the numerous pilot programs and tests conducted across major Chinese cities like Shenzhen, Suzhou, and Chengdu. These trials, involving millions of citizens, businesses, and public services, reveal the government's determination to embed the digital yuan into the fabric of daily life in China. In fact, starting in May 2023, the Chinese City of Changshu will begin paying employees using the digital yuan. The 261 million CBDC wallets in China today will expand to reach the rest of the population by the end of 2023.

The Dark Side of Nigeria's CBDC: Privacy, Tyranny, and a Cautionary Tale

The IMF, you will recall from chapter 3, is a centralized force in the global financial system, that wielded its influence to push a centralized CBDC program onto Nigeria, and the outcome has been nothing short of disastrous. The eNaira, Nigeria's new digital currency, was launched in October 2021 under the guidance of the IMF, which provided technical assistance, policy guidance, and expertise. Its aim was to ensure that Nigeria's Central Bank conformed to a centralized, tightly-controlled financial system. The eNaira was intended to revolutionize Nigeria's economy and promote financial inclusion, but the centralized agenda led to unintended consequences that have disrupted the lives of ordinary Nigerians.

Following the launch of the eNaira, the Nigerian government implemented cash restrictions to accelerate the transition to a cashless society, leading to a cash shortage and widespread frustration among the populace. Citizens, angered by the lack of physical cash and the forced adoption of a digital currency, took to the streets in protest. The civil unrest escalated, as incidents of violence and chaos emerged in response to the government's failure to recognize the importance of cash in the lives of its people.

The eNaira's adoption, driven by the IMF's imposition of its centralized vision, has raised serious concerns about the erosion of privacy and the potential for increased government surveillance. CBDCs like the eNaira can track every transaction, providing a wealth of data that allows intrusive governments to scrutinize citizens' lives. The situation in Nigeria echoes the concerns raised by China's digital yuan, which has been widely criticized for its potential to enable a surveillance state.

The disastrous consequences of the IMF's involvement in Nigeria should serve as a stark warning for the rest of the world. The sense of shock, anger, and concern that has arisen from the eNaira debacle underlines the importance of remaining vigilant against the rapid imposition of centralized CBDC programs, which could lead to similar disastrous outcomes in the US and beyond.

CBDCs Coming to America

The US stands at a critical juncture, as the government's pursuit of CBDCs gains unprecedented momentum. Within the next 12 months, the cherished American ideal of freedom could be undermined by a centrally controlled digital currency. Unbeknownst to many, the Federal Reserve has already conducted three successful wide-ranging CBDC pilots, while President Joe Biden has championed the cause through the sweeping Executive Order 14067. This order has set in motion a multi-agency effort to lay the foundation for digital currencies, bringing the dystopian scenarios outlined in earlier chapters closer to reality.

In this section, we will examine President Biden's Executive Order, delve into the three CBDC pilot programs, and explore the implications of the forthcoming FedNow infrastructure, set to launch nationwide in July 2023, which could enable the rapid deployment of CBDCs in the US. The situation is more dire than it even appears on the surface, as they want to be able to not only control and program money but also digital assets. Imagine if stocks, bonds, homes, cars, computers, literally any assets could be tracked centrally by the government and the sale or transfer of those assets could be blocked by multiple 3rd parties (including the government, Federal Reserve, and other centralized

3rd parties). The shock, alarm, and anger provoked by these revelations should serve as a rallying cry for those seeking alternatives, striving to share this crucial information and take action to stop this before it's too late.

Executive Order 14067

On March 9, 2022, President Biden signed Executive Order 14067, "Ensuring Responsible Development of Digital Assets." The order directs the US government to take a whole-of-government approach to the development of digital assets, including CBDCs. The order is expansive in its scope, covering a wide range of issues related to digital assets, including their potential impact on the financial system, national security, and consumer protection. The order also directs the US government to work with international partners to develop responsible standards for digital assets (enter UN, WEF, IMF, World Bank, and BIS).

Jim Rickards, a respected expert on financial markets and geopolitics, has sounded the alarm bell about the significant problems and overreach in this Executive Order. He believes that the order is too broad and does not provide enough guidance on how the government should develop and implement a CBDC. He is also concerned that the order could lead to the erosion of privacy and financial sovereignty. Rickards explains, "Executive Order 14067 is a dangerous step towards a cashless society. It gives the government too much power to track and control our financial transactions." He further adds "The order is also a threat to privacy and financial sovereignty. It could lead to the erosion of our right to control our own money."

To be very clear, the President of the United States has put forward a framework that looks like the dystopian nightmare we are so desperately trying to avoid. Rickard warns, "The order is a missed opportunity to promote innovation and competition in the payments system. Instead, it is a recipe for government control and surveillance."

US CBDC Pilot Programs

Even prior to Biden's Executive Order, the Federal Reserve was well underway in researching, developing, and piloting CBDCs.

Let's take a closer look at the key CBDC initiatives: Project Hamilton, Project Cedar, the Regulated Liability Network (RLN) program, and FedNow and explore what they mean for the future of money and personal freedom in the United States.

Project Hamilton

Project Hamilton, a joint venture between the Federal Reserve Bank of Boston and MIT, explored the use of a retail CBDC during a pilot program that ran from 2020-2022. A retail CBDC is a digital form of fiat currency that is issued by a central bank (in this case the Federal Reserve) and can be accessed directly by the public. This form of electronic cash would replace the dollar and would be used to make payments, saved, or used to make investments. A recently published whitepaper details the pilot program's results, which include signs that a digital dollar can handle a large number of transactions safely and securely. The pilot managed to process approximately 1.7 million transactions per second at its fastest. By comparison, the current US banking system can only handle 150,000 transactions per second. Clearly, this new CBDC has the technical capacity to replace the existing financial infrastructure.

The group heading up Project Hamilton, the MIT Digital Currency Initiative, received funding from the MIT Media Lab whose big-name donors, Bill Gates, and Jeffrey Epstein, reveal a globalist agenda that seeks to centralize power and undermine individual autonomy. Both Joi Ito (the former head of the MIT Media Lab) and Bill Gates made multiple trips to Epstein's notorious Island. This is the dystopian nightmare we've warned about – and it's unfolding right before our eyes.

Project Cedar

Contrasting with other initiatives, Project Cedar sets its sights on investigating the potential applications and use cases of a CBDC specifically within the context of the wholesale market. This project is a joint venture involving the Federal Reserve Bank of New York, several prominent banking institutions, namely JPMorgan Chase, Bank of New York Mellon, and State Street, along with the BIS and the MIT Media Lab, which also played a role in Project Hamilton.

To better understand, the wholesale market refers to a financial environment where transactions are typically large in scale and high in value, conducted predominantly between financial institutions like banks, businesses, and other financial entities. It's a behind-the-scenes arena where substantial monetary exchanges take place, far from the realm of individual or retail transactions.

Thus, the primary audience for Project Cedar encompasses the financial institutions and stakeholders who operate within this wholesale market. The goal of the project is to comprehend how a digital dollar could be utilized in this setting, facilitating these significant transactions efficiently, securely, and seamlessly.

As part of the pilot program, Project Cedar scrutinizes numerous aspects of a wholesale CBDC. This includes the technology's capacity to enable instantaneous, secure settlements between institutions, the potential regulatory challenges that may arise, and the compatibility of the digital dollar with the existing financial infrastructure.

Technically speaking, the pilot program has been successful, paving the way towards the next phase of the project: selling the concept to the public and gaining consensus among central banks.

Regulated Liability Network (RLN)

In addition to Project Cedar (which is in its second pilot phase) the Federal Reserve Bank of New York is also involved in another pilot called the Regulated Liability Network (RLN) that "will participate in a proof-of-concept project to explore the feasibility of an interoperable network of central bank wholesale digital money and commercial bank digital money operating on a shared multi-entity distributed ledger."

What does this mean, exactly? Imagine a future where every asset you buy (stocks, bonds, homes, cars, electronics, jewelry, etc.) are issued as digital tokens that can be tracked and settled by the government and other third parties through a centralized framework. In addition to being able to censor and freeze your money if you don't behave the way those in control demand, they can also block the sale and perhaps even the use of your assets. Imagine that you buy a computer with a CBDC. A digital token is created that is associated with that computer. If you engaged in behavior that the authorities didn't like, they could track your computer and remotely disable your ability to use it or sell it. In chapter one we discussed how the government could control your UBI based on your social credit score. With something like the RLN, they could also potentially block your ability to sell your car, home, or even impair your ability to use your assets remotely through this type of digital asset tracking and remote monitoring.

Like the other two pilot programs, the RLN pilot has ties to globalist organizations including the BIS and the MIT Media Lab (who is involved with all 3 CBDC pilots). "The RLN pilot is a collaboration between a number of leading financial institutions, regulators, and technology providers. It is a significant step forward in the development of a regulated digital asset ecosystem." - MIT Media Lab

FedNow

As we shift our focus to FedNow, it's crucial to understand the impending impact of this instant payment platform, slated for a nationwide launch in July 2023. Developed by the Federal Reserve, FedNow aims to revolutionize the way financial institutions settle transactions by providing real-time gross settlement services. In today's world, clearing a check can take up to a week, ACH transfers between banks require 1-3 days, and even wire transfers aren't instantaneous – not to mention they can cost $20-$30 per transaction.

Enter FedNow – a game-changing system that will facilitate instantaneous payments, 24/7/365, at a mere fraction of a cent per transaction. While it's essential to note that FedNow is not a CBDC itself, its significance cannot be understated. This innovative platform could very well serve as the critical infrastructure that enables CBDCs to seamlessly integrate into the financial landscape. So, as we dive deeper into the world of FedNow, remember the potential it holds to usher in a new era of digital currency.

The Fed is very serious about the importance of this program, and they seem to be willing to take extreme efforts to protect their monopoly position. Early this year, two of the banks that collapsed (Signature Bank and Silvergate Bank) had settlement solutions that competed directly with FedNow. Signature Bank had an offering called Signet and Silvergate had an offering called Sentral. Whereas Silvergate Bank failed largely due to its association with FTX and other failed crypto entities, it could be argued that the deposit run on Signature Bank was engineered by word being leaked that some of their crypto clients were being investigated by the SEC (nothing was mentioned about any specific clients just rumors of a broad-based SEC investigation) – causing a run on the bank.

As part of the deal to acquire Signature Bank, the acquirer, BNY Mellon (a large financial services company with $46.6 trillion of assets under custody/management), had to agree not to be involved in crypto for a period of five years. Regulators used the excuse that BNY's involvement in crypto could pose a risk to the stability of the financial system. It also, conveniently, gives the Federal Reserve the opportunity to launch FedNow without competition. Many from the Federal Reserve and the CEO of the Digital Dollar Project have discussed the potential use of FedNow as a launchpad for a CBDC, "FedNow has the potential to be a valuable infrastructure for a CBDC. It could provide a secure and efficient platform for the issuance, distribution, and settlement of CBDCs."

Let me summarize where the US is with respect to CBDCs:

- Project Hamilton is a successful pilot of a retail CBDC that could replace the dollar for day-to-day transactions. This system can handle more than 3x the transaction volume of the existing banking system.
- Project Cedar is a successful pilot wholesale CBDC trial that makes it faster and cheaper for financial institutions to transact with each other, with an emphasis on transferring funds between financial institutions located in different countries.
- Regulated Liability Network: is a pilot program that would allow for the centralization and control of both CBDCs and digital assets (stocks, bonds, homes, etc.) by multiple centralized 3rd parties.
- FedNow: Real-time settlement will go live for business and consumers in the US in July 2023. This infrastructure could be potentially used to roll out CBDCs in the future.

CBDC isn't coming, it's already here. At this point it is just a matter of time until it is rolled out -unless we stop it. Waiting is not an effective strategy. I have heard many people argue that we shouldn't exit the banks and move into self-custody crypto, gold, or silver because it will speed up the implementation of CBDC. Those who hold this view are oblivious of how far CBDCs have progressed. The technology is on the shelf waiting for an emergency to usher it in. The only way we stop CBDC is by exiting the existing system BEFORE they get the infrastructure in place. This is why the back half of this book provides an overview of self-custody crypto, gold, and silver and how you can take immediate action.

You might be thinking that you just want things to go back to the way they were before COVID and before all this discussion of CBDCs and digital currency. I assure you, there is no scenario where this is possible. You will be surprised to learn that the dollar's demise is inevitable as well. As we will see in the next chapter, fiat currencies (backed nothing but trust in a government's ability to pay its debts) have failed throughout history. There are no exceptions, and the US Dollar is flashing all the warning signs of a fiat currency in collapse. What CBDCs offer is just a technical and more centralized version of fiat currency. In the end, fiat currencies don't work (despite being tried thousands of times). We need a new model. We need to separate money and government. The time to embrace self-custody crypto, gold, and silver is now. We must resist the encroaching digital dollar and its Orwellian implications for society.

Key takeaways from Chapter 4:

- China's digital yuan carries the potential for increased government surveillance and control, leading to a loss of privacy and autonomy.
- Nigeria's eNaira serves as a cautionary tale, with brave and determined citizens protesting the push for a cashless society and its potential for privacy invasion and tyranny.
- The U.S. government is accelerating its efforts to implement a CBDC through initiatives like Project Hamilton and Project Cedar.
- Globalist organizations and agendas are influencing the development of CBDCs, bent on undermining individual freedom and autonomy.

- CBDCs, as centralized versions of fiat currencies, pose an existential threat to humanity. No one should have all their eggs in one basket.
- Embracing self-custody crypto, gold, and silver is crucial to resist centralized control and protect personal freedom.
- Separation of money and state is a vital principle to uphold in the fight against CBDCs.
- CBDCs are gaining traction worldwide, with various countries at different stages of development and implementation.
- The challenges and concerns surrounding CBDCs are not isolated to specific countries, but rather represent a global trend toward centralized control.

Artwork:

"Paper money eventually returns to its intrinsic value –
zero." - Voltaire

Oh, fiat currencies, a tale so dire,
With every rise, they're bound to expire.
From ancient Rome to present day,
Their fate remains the same, we say.

The Dollar's end may soon be near,
A truth we must confront, and fear.
In El Salvador, Bitcoin's rise,
A glimpse of hope, a new sunrise.

United we must stand, as one,
Self-custody our wealth, begun.
With gold and silver, crypto too,
Together we'll prevail, anew.

Chapter 5: The Inevitable Downfall of Fiat Currencies: Lessons from History and a Call to Action

The notion that the dollar, the reigning global currency, could falter seems unfathomable to most of us. However, in this chapter, we will challenge this comforting illusion. History is unambiguous: every fiat currency, backed by nothing more than faith in governmental solvency, has ultimately failed. The US Dollar is no exception. At present, we're witnessing telltale signs of impending currency collapse, with major bank failures and estimates suggesting up to half of US banks teetering on insolvency. We've outpaced the 2008 crisis, and we aren't even in a recession yet!

In preceding chapters, we've presented a grim prospect of imminent CBDCs and their potential threats to our liberties. However, let's not harbor illusions of reverting to a pre-COVID financial utopia. Our journey towards a digital monetary future is inevitable. Will we adopt a CBDC (essentially a digital avatar of fiat currency), or will we defy historical precedent, separating money from government power, and chart a decentralized course?

In this chapter, we'll guide you through the labyrinth of fiat currency, its turbulent chronicle, and the inescapable destiny awaiting every paper empire. We'll delve into history, examining the collapse of Rome, the financial chaos in Berlin, contemporary Argentinean economic woes, and even the bold Bitcoin experiment in El Salvador, our first real-world test case for the separation of money and government.

We'll scrutinize the U.S. dollar's trajectory from modest origins to global supremacy, revealing the cracks beneath its formidable façade that forecast its downfall.

By the end of this chapter, the inevitability of the dollar's decline will be apparent. The architects of fiat currency have deftly manipulated a problem-reaction-solution strategy: induce a financial system collapse, amplify fear, and then present the CBDCs as the antidote, further consolidating their control.

Yet, hope endures for those willing to explore alternative paths. The window is narrowing, and we must act swiftly, embracing self-custody crypto, gold, and silver. As the shadow of CBDC looms, transitioning from fiat to self-custody alternatives may be our sole defense against absolute tyranny. Knowledge is our weapon, and we're about to empower you with a potent arsenal of truths that will, at the very least, give you a fighting chance.

Why This Chapter Matters

Comprehending the unavoidable failure of fiat currencies is essential in steering clear of the shortcomings that have led to their demise time and time again. Analyzing currency collapses from ancient Rome to contemporary Zimbabwe uncovers the inherent defects present in all fiat systems. Being aware of the dollar's susceptibility allows us to take proactive financial steps by diversifying into self-custody options before its decline worsens.

El Salvador's Bitcoin experiment highlights the potential for promising alternatives. This understanding encourages us to maintain a skeptical attitude towards endeavors to supplant faltering fiat systems with centralized digital currencies. In doing so, we can advocate for solutions that genuinely uphold individual freedom and autonomy.

A Brief History of Fiat Currency and some Notable Major Failures

As we embark on this historical odyssey of fiat currency, let us first acknowledge the inherent flaws of this human-made invention. Fiat currencies, those colorful papers we've grown so attached to, have a notorious reputation for biting the dust. In fact, the average lifespan of a fiat currency is a mere 27 years. This section will shed light on the rise and fall of these ill-fated monetary systems.

Throughout history, civilizations have experimented with various forms of currency, from seashells to precious metals. However, it wasn't until the advent of fiat money that societies truly flirted with economic disaster. To date, an astonishing number of fiat currencies (literally thousands) have existed, each meeting their untimely demise due to a myriad of factors.

What is fiat money/currency? Fiat money/currency is a government-issued currency that is not backed by a physical commodity, such as gold or silver, but rather by the government that issued it. The US dollar is fiat money, as are the currencies of most countries.

Enter the realm of Mike Hewitt, the intrepid author of "DollarDaze: A History of Fiat Currency Failures." Hewitt dared to analyze 750 fiat currencies in his groundbreaking work. Through meticulous research, he uncovered the patterns and pitfalls that led to their downfall. His findings, a veritable treasure trove of monetary misfortune, can be distilled into seven key reasons for failure:

- Excessive debt
- Economic mismanagement
- Political instability
- Hyperinflation
- Loss of confidence
- Currency competition
- War and conflict

Despite our modern advancements, the same old ghosts continue to haunt today's fiat currencies. In recent years, we've witnessed a surge in hyperinflation events, driven by the same root causes that have plagued currencies for centuries.

We'll delve into five harrowing tales of fiat currency catastrophes. Each story, a cautionary tale, will illustrate the common themes and consequences of a currency's untimely demise. From the ashes of Rome to the smoldering ruins of Berlin, and to the tragic fate of Argentina, we'll glean valuable insights into the dangers that lurk within the world of fiat.

Rome

Our journey begins with the tale of the Roman Denarius. Picture, if you will, the golden age of the Roman Empire, with its far-reaching boundaries extending across the then-known world. The Empire's supremacy paralleled the current dominance of the United States.

The Denarius, a gleaming silver coin, was the heartbeat of the Roman economy, facilitating trade, taxes, and tributes. Introduced in 211 BCE, it became a pillar of Rome's financial system, symbolizing wealth and power that echoed throughout the empire. But this beloved currency, unbeknownst to Romans, was headed towards a fate that would foretell calamity.

As Rome's aspirations expanded, so did its resource requirements. The empire began overreaching, and its leaders resorted to a perilous practice of monetary manipulation. The Denarius, once a lustrous emblem of stability, was gradually diluted by the infusion of base metals like copper. This process permitted the production of more coins from the same quantity of silver, deceptively maintaining the coin's face value while reducing its intrinsic value. This slow erosion of the currency's worth resembles termites silently compromising the structure of a grand edifice.

Debasement of the Denarius triggered adverse consequences.

Rome soon grappled with issues typically associated with the collapse of fiat currencies. Let's recount the empire's transgressions:

- Excessive debt and unfunded liabilities – Rome's military expeditions, extravagant public works and pension obligations severely depleted the treasury.
- Economic mismanagement – Constant meddling with the Denarius by the government wreaked havoc on the economy.
- Political instability – A succession of emperors and power-seekers added to the empire's instability.

Thus, the stage was set for catastrophe. By the 3rd century CE, the once-glorious Denarius had been debased to less than 0.5% silver content. This debasement ignited rampant inflation, as prices skyrocketed, and citizens grappled with dwindling resources. The previously prosperous Roman economy faltered, signaling the empire's descent.

The fall of the Denarius sent tremors throughout the ancient world, forever reshaping history's course. The decline of Rome was punctuated by its territories' fragmentation, as the once-unified empire disintegrated into a mosaic of feuding factions. This tumultuous period, characterized by the rise of barbarian kingdoms and dwindling central authority, set the stage for the Middle Ages. Within the tragic narrative of the Roman Denarius, we find a warning and a parallel to our own potential demise.

Germany

Next, we turn our attention to the turbulent times of post-World War I Germany, an era marked by the punishing burden of war reparations and the notorious Treaty of Versailles. Let's explore the saga of the German Papiermark, a poignant narrative of hyperinflation and economic disaster.

In many ways akin to the present-day United States, Germany in the early 20th century was a hub of industry and innovation. However, the devastating aftermath of the Great War left the nation in ruins, its economy on the brink of collapse. Into this chaos stepped the Papiermark, the contemporary German currency, oblivious of its impending status as the epitome of hyperinflation.

The story of the Papiermark's collapse is a grim tale of desperation and despair. With war reparations bleeding the national treasury dry and political pressure intensifying, the German government succumbed to the dangerous strategy of unrestrained money printing. This critical misstep triggered a cascade of catastrophic events, etching the Papiermark's name into the hall of monetary infamy.

Germany's journey towards ruin echoed the factors that have precipitated fiat currency failures throughout history. As we delve into the Papiermark's downfall's grim narrative, let's recount the country's missteps:

> • Unchecked money supply - The government's relentless money printing stoked the flames of hyperinflation.
> • Loss of confidence - As the Papiermark's value nose-dived, so did the German populace's trust in their currency.

• Economic mismanagement - The government's inability to address the root causes of hyperinflation only accelerated the Papiermark's decline.

During the height of the Papiermark hyperinflation, the German people found themselves in a surreal nightmare. What was once a comfortable middle-class family could suddenly find themselves on the brink of destitution. Savings that took a lifetime to amass turned into mere pocket change overnight. Stories abound of families carrying wheelbarrows full of Papiermarks to buy a loaf of bread, only to find that the price had doubled by the time they reached the store. People were burning stacks of currency for warmth as it was cheaper than buying firewood. In one poignant account, a woman who had left her wheelbarrow filled with cash outside a shop returned to find the money untouched, but the wheelbarrow stolen. Such was the worthless nature of the Papiermark at the time. This hyperinflationary period left an indelible scar on the psyche of the German people, a chilling reminder of how quickly a currency's value can evaporate and the devastating human cost it can inflict.

Zimbabwe

We now set our sights on the alluring landscapes of Zimbabwe, an African nation teeming with natural splendor and abundant resources. Despite its earthly gifts, Zimbabwe stands as a stark reminder of the devastation that economic calamity can wreak, etched forever in the annals of history through the tale of the infamous Zimbabwe Dollar.

As the 20th century drew to a close, Zimbabwe was caught in a maelstrom of economic missteps and pervasive corruption, striking parallels to the tribulations the United States confronts today. With its economy in freefall, the Zimbabwe Dollar found itself on a disastrous path to oblivion.

The saga of the Zimbabwe Dollar is one of staggering proportions. With the government's printing presses running amok, the value of the currency plummeted at a breathtaking pace. Prices spiraled out of control, leading to scenarios so absurd they bordered on the farcical. Picture the following everyday predicaments:

- Carting groceries to the counter with wheelbarrows filled with cash, only to find the prices had doubled by the time you reached the cashier.
- Barely keeping up with the escalating cost of a bus ride, with fares shooting up by the minute.
- The Zimbabwean Stock Exchange turning into the world's best-performing market, not due to stellar investments, but as a byproduct of rampant inflation.

In its downfall, the Zimbabwe Dollar bore the unmistakable hallmarks that have preceded the collapse of numerous fiat currencies throughout history:

- Unchecked money printing - The government's relentless money printing expedited the spiral into hyperinflation.
- Evaporation of faith - As the Zimbabwe Dollar's value plummeted, so did the people's trust in their currency.
- Economic mismanagement - The government's inability to address the root causes of hyperinflation sealed the currency's fate.

As we delve into the aftermath of the Zimbabwe Dollar's collapse, we encounter a panorama of hardship and despair. The once prosperous nation, brimming with potential, was reduced to an economic wasteland. Poverty became the unwelcome guest at every doorstep, and food shortages transformed meals into rare luxuries.

Consider this chilling anecdote of a Zimbabwean school teacher: Once a respected professional, she found herself struggling to feed her family. Her monthly salary, once sufficient, turned into a cruel joke as prices skyrocketed. She would receive her salary in the morning, and by afternoon, the prices would have already doubled, rendering her earnings practically worthless. This was a daily struggle, a frantic race against inflation, where the finish line kept moving further away.

Meanwhile, the now-obsolete Zimbabwe Dollar found a bizarre second life as a symbol of extreme hyperinflation. The infamous 100 trillion Zimbabwe Dollar bill, once a symbol of economic despair, became a collector's item and an internet sensation. But behind this oddity lies a sobering reminder of the catastrophic consequences of unchecked economic mismanagement, a timeless warning for all nations.

Argentina

Let's now set our sights on the vibrant land of tango, dulce de leche, and a currency grappling with dramatic upheaval - Argentina. The Argentine Peso, the fiscal heart of this once-flourishing South American nation, has been caught in a whirlwind of economic turbulence, enduring multiple crises throughout its history.

The story of the Argentine Peso is a stark tale of fiscal missteps, economic recklessness, and rapid currency devaluation. As inflation rates skyrocketed, hitting a staggering 100% in February 2023, the Argentine government found itself in a desperate race against time, attempting to stem a tide that had already wreaked havoc.

Picture the day-to-day realities for the Argentine population during these tumultuous times:

- Experiencing the shock of your morning coffee's price doubling overnight, making you question the worth of this simple pleasure.
- Hastening to the supermarket at the first hint of a price hike, only to be greeted by empty shelves, picked clean by fellow worried citizens.
- Turning to the underground economy to exchange your swiftly devaluing pesos for a more stable currency, all the while wary of the authorities' gaze.

The Argentine Peso's precarious journey bears striking similarities to other fiat currency collapses:

- Economic imprudence - The Argentine government has repeatedly fallen prey to reckless spending and escalating debt.
- Eroding trust - As inflation spiraled, so did public confidence in the peso's ability to retain value.
- Counterproductive policies - Governmental attempts to curb inflation often worsened the situation, adding fuel to the fire.

The collapse of the Argentine Peso has had profound repercussions, spawning economic instability, rampant poverty, societal upheaval, and political turmoil. However, in this maelstrom, Argentinians have discovered an unexpected ally in the form of cryptocurrency. The International Monetary Fund (IMF) has been implicated in Argentina's currency crisis, further engendering mistrust, and catalyzing the population's shift towards digital alternatives.

Back in 1991, the IMF extended a $50 billion loan to Argentina to steady its economy. This financial lifeline, however, came attached with austerity measures, culminating in cuts to government spending and social programs. These cutbacks, coupled with other factors, precipitated Argentina's 2001 recession. As the peso's value plummeted, the country defaulted on its debt.

Adding to this controversy, the IMF stands accused of attempting to ban Bitcoin in Argentina. In a 2019 report, the organization proposed regulating Bitcoin as a "financial activity," citing worries over potential illicit usage. Despite this, Bitcoin's popularity in Argentina surged, as illustrated by the doubling of Bitcoin ATMs in the country in 2021.

As the Argentine peso nosedived, cryptocurrencies like Bitcoin emerged as a financial sanctuary, enabling citizens to shield their savings from inflation and execute international payments without traditional banking institutions. The IMF's alleged involvement in Argentina's currency collapse has only amplified the allure of digital currencies, providing a financial beacon during these challenging times.

In an environment rife with distrust and disillusionment, cryptocurrencies offer a glimmer of hope and stability for Argentinians eager to secure their financial future. As the economist Javier Milei notes, "The IMF's intervention in Argentina has had a series of adverse effects. It has led to austerity measures that have detrimentally impacted the poor and middle class. It has also resulted in a loss of faith in the government and the financial system. This has propelled the demand for Bitcoin, which is perceived as a means to safeguard savings from inflation and governmental control."

In a bold move to combat soaring inflation rates, the Central Bank of Argentina has raised its key interest rate by six points to a staggering 97%. This decisive action comes as the nation grapples with the worst inflation in three decades, which hit over 100% last month (April 2023), marking the third highest globally, trailing only Venezuela and Zimbabwe.

The Central Bank hopes to ignite investment in the nation's currency, countering the drastic inflation that led to significant investment outflows from the Argentine peso and a 23% depreciation against the US dollar this year.

Simultaneously, the political scenario is heating up with Economy Minister Sergio Massa, who aims to stem further currency devaluation and control inflation, potentially standing as a third-party candidate in the upcoming October presidential elections. However, critics, including former deputy manager at the Central Bank of Argentina, Miguel Kiguel, caution that the dramatic rate increase may not be the immediate remedy the Argentinian markets need, suggesting it could be a case of too little, too late.

El Salvador

Venturing northwest from Argentina, we reach our final case study — El Salvador. Prior to the reign of the dollar, El Salvador relied on its national currency, the Salvadoran colón. However, in a bid to stabilize the economy, attract foreign investments, and curb inflation, the country opted to abandon the colón in favor of the US dollar in 2001. But, as it turned out, the greener pastures of the dollar held their own set of challenges. Let's explore five key issues that El Salvador faced under the dollar regime:

- Monetary policy restrictions: Dollar adoption implied that El Salvador was at the mercy of US monetary policies, bereft of any control over its own interest rates or the flexibility to adjust exchange rates in response to economic fluctuations.
- Currency discrepancy: The lion's share of El Salvador's external debt was denominated in US dollars, complicating the management of their debt obligations.
- Stunted economic growth: The rigidity of the dollarized economy hindered El Salvador's ability to address structural problems and promote sustainable growth.
- Expanding wealth disparity: The affluent urbanites were the primary beneficiaries of dollarization, while the rural and impoverished communities were largely left in the lurch.
- Exposure to external factors: The nation's dependency on the US dollar made it susceptible to the whims of the US economy and currency valuation.

The International Monetary Fund (IMF) aired its apprehensions about El Salvador's financial stability, urging the government to intervene. Enter Bitcoin — the digital gold rush that ignited a revolution. El Salvador's President, Nayib Bukele, recognized Bitcoin's potential to tackle these issues and more. In September 2021, the country officially welcomed Bitcoin as legal tender, sharing the stage with the US dollar. This audacious move was met with both hope and skepticism. As the saying goes, fortune does indeed favor the bold.

Bitcoin adoption promised a host of benefits for El Salvador, such as financial inclusivity, reduced dependency on remittances, and a boost in foreign investments. The journey has seen highs and lows, yet the nation stands firmly committed to cryptocurrency. As one excited Chivo wallet user put it, "Bitcoin has unlocked new avenues and financial liberty for the people." However, the sentiment isn't universal. A disgruntled citizen noted, "It's been a wild ride, with Bitcoin's volatile value causing hiccups for small businesses and everyday transactions."

Recent advancements in El Salvador's Bitcoin experiment encompass the passage of a law regulating cryptocurrency transactions, evolving tactics during the 2022 bear market, and the abolition of all taxes related to technological innovation to spur economic growth. While the country's daring move has captured global headlines, only time will bear witness to its success. An old Salvadoran proverb states, "No risk, no gain." For now, it seems, El Salvador is playing for high stakes.

The outcome for El Salvador remains uncertain, but it is noteworthy that they are attempting something novel — transitioning away from a state-sponsored fiat currency. Given the historical failure of all fiat currencies, it's a gamble worth taking.

Fiat Currency in the United States

We've surveyed the landscape from a broad perspective, demonstrating the undeniable pattern of fiat currency failures throughout history. We've illuminated various narratives from disparate timelines and corners of the globe, all culminating in the inescapable downward spiral of fiat currencies. As it turns out, the dollar is not an exception to this rule, sharing the fate of its ill-starred predecessors. In the forthcoming section, we're going to delve deeper into this phenomenon as it pertains to the dollar.

Global Reserve Currency Status Doesn't Last Forever

For anyone born post-1920, the US dollar's status as the global reserve currency is a lifelong given. This familiarity often leads to the assumption that the dollar's dominance is a timeless, unchanging truth. However, a stroll through the corridors of history offers a starkly contrasting narrative.

Global Reserve Currency	Country	Years Active	Duration
US Dollar	USA	1920-present	103+ years
Pound Sterling	United Kingdom	1815-1920	105 years
French franc	France	1720-1815	95 years
Dutch Guilder	Dutch Republic	1640-1720	80 years
Spanish Dollar	Spain	1530-1640	110 years
Portuguese real	Portugal	1450-1530	80 years

As illustrated by the above table, while there tends to be a prevailing currency, the reign as the global reserve is usually transient, typically concluding after approximately a century. The US dollar has held this prestigious title for 103 years, suggesting, based on historical patterns, that its era of dominance is nearing its twilight. This is increasingly apparent as nations like Brazil, Russia, India, China, and others are steadily pivoting away from using the dollar for international trade.

The History of the Dollar in America

The dollar, as we know it, wasn't always America's currency. In fact, the country has weathered numerous currency failures, and some might argue that our current dollar, based on a central banking system, could be the most deceptive one yet. Let's take a brief journey back in time to understand the evolution of American currencies before the advent of modern central banking:

- Continental Currency (1775-1789): Introduced to finance the Revolutionary War, Continental Currency was plagued by uncontrolled inflation due to excessive printing and the absence of gold or silver backing. The currency eventually became worthless, leading to the origin of the phrase "not worth a Continental."
- State Banknotes (1780s-1860s): These banknotes were circulated by individual banks, causing inconsistencies in their value and a surge in counterfeiting. The chaos that ensued led to numerous financial panics and collapses.
- The First and Second Banks of the United States (1791-1811 and 1816-1836): Both institutions faced stiff opposition from critics who perceived them as tools for the affluent to manipulate the economy. The charter of the Second Bank wasn't renewed, giving way to the "Free Banking Era," a period marked by countless bank failures and economic instability.

113

The Federal Reserve and the Era of Modern Banking

"It is well enough that people of the nation do not understand our banking and monetary system, for if they did, I believe there would be a revolution before tomorrow morning." -Henry Ford

Moving forward from these historical failures, we now enter the contemporary era with a currency that we're all well acquainted with – one built on the model of central banking. The Federal Reserve, often abbreviated as the Fed, is the central banking system of the United States. However, even the term "Federal Reserve" can be misleading. Despite the name, the Fed isn't a federal institution in the conventional sense, nor does it hold "reserves" in the traditional banking sense.

Founded in 1913, the Fed operates with a degree of independence from the government, meaning it doesn't rely on Congress for funding nor is it directly accountable to politicians. Its principal declared mission is to regulate the country's monetary policy, foster financial stability, and ensure a robust economy. This involves curbing inflation, managing interest rates, and supervising the banking system. In actuality, it is a system governed by private banks, where these banks conjure up money based on federal government IOUs (which are required to be repaid to the Federal Reserve with interest).

A captivating account of the history and establishment of the Federal Reserve is encapsulated in the book "The Creature from Jekyll Island."

- Clandestine Gathering: The inception of the Federal Reserve System was shrouded in secrecy, taking place in a covert meeting on

Jekyll Island, Georgia, in 1910. Here, powerful bankers and politicians conspired to formulate a centralized banking system, far from public scrutiny.

• Fabricated Solution: The justification for the establishment of the Fed was to supposedly avert recurring banking crises prevalent in the late 19th and early 20th centuries. The architects behind the Federal Reserve Act understood the potential of crisis exploitation all too well.

• Enshrined in Law: With the Federal Reserve Act of 1913, the United States witnessed the birth of the Federal Reserve System as the ultimate banking authority.

• Control Under Guise: The Fed comprises 12 regional banks, privately owned by their member banks. This structure masks the influence of private banks over the central banking system under a veneer of independence and decentralization, allowing private banks to profit from the system they effectively control.

• Misleading Independence: Despite assertions of operating independently from the government, the Fed's primary source of revenue is the interest on government securities - essentially IOUs. Thus, the Fed's profits increase in direct proportion to the amount the Federal Government borrows, creating a conflict of interest.

• Monetary Manipulation: The Fed dictates the nation's monetary policy, adjusting interest rates and managing the money supply, ostensibly to foster economic stability and growth.

• Elastic Currency: The Fed holds the authority to create an 'elastic currency,' which can be expanded or contracted based on economic conditions, a power criticized for its propensity to cause inflation or devalue the currency.

• Taxation Nexus: The inception of the federal income tax and IRS coincided with the formation of the Federal Reserve. In essence, the IRS acts as an armed collection agency, funded by taxpayers, whose purpose is to collect principal and interest for private banks on money conjured from thin air and backed by government IOUs.

• Engineered Wealth Redistribution: The Fed's policies facilitate wealth redistribution, disproportionately favoring certain entities such as large corporations and banks, while disadvantaging others, notably small businesses and the average citizen.

The Dollar and the Gold Standard

In our world's financial history, the gold standard played a key role as a monetary system wherein the value of a country's currency was directly anchored to a specific quantity of gold. For the United States, this meant that every unit of the dollar had a corresponding value in gold, maintaining a fixed exchange rate.

Starting in the early 20th century, the United States operated under the gold standard, and this dictated that the price of gold was $20.67 per ounce. This all changed in 1934 with the implementation of the Gold Reserve

Act. This piece of legislation redefined the value of the dollar, essentially devaluing it. The government set a new rate, stipulating that one ounce of gold was equivalent to $35, not the previous $20.67. This pivot was a significant devaluation of the dollar, with the direct aim to stimulate the economy during the Great Depression by making gold more expensive and hence, making the dollar more attractive.

While the US officially stepped away from the domestic gold standard in 1933, it did not entirely abandon the principle. Instead, it shifted to a more nuanced system known as the Bretton Woods System, which was in place from 1944 to 1971. Under this arrangement, the US dollar was still tied to gold, but with a twist. While the dollar continued to be pegged to a fixed amount of gold, the currencies of other nations were now pegged to the value of the US dollar.

This essentially meant that the value of other world currencies was indirectly linked to gold through their relationship with the dollar. The US dollar became the primary reserve currency, acting as the global economic fulcrum. This system of monetary management established the rules for commercial and financial relations among the world's major industrial states, promoting monetary cooperation and economic stability. However, this system ended in 1971, marking the departure from the gold standard completely.

In essence, when a currency is "pegged," it is directly linked or tied to another asset's value. In this historical context, the dollar was pegged to gold, and subsequently, other currencies were pegged to the dollar, creating a global financial network of interconnected value.

Nixon abandons the gold standard

In 1971, a historic event unfolded as the US abandoned the gold standard, cutting off the dollar's tether to gold. This move, orchestrated by President Nixon, sent seismic ripples through global financial markets. Countries worldwide scrambled to recalibrate their economies, many grappling with currency devaluations, inflation, and economic chaos. Thus, the era of fiat money was ushered in. To recap the situation by 1971, the dollar's journey had seen it transition from being gold-backed, to being pegged to gold at $35 an ounce, to having all global currencies pegged to a dollar that was itself pegged to gold, to the dollar finally breaking free of its gold connection altogether. At this juncture, the dollar was backed solely by government IOUs. The same government that hasn't had a balanced budget since 2001 and has a national debt of $32 Trillion dollars (up from $5.7 Trillion in 2001). Sounds ominous, doesn't it? Brace yourself, the plot thickens.

Fractional reserve banking

Banks function using a system known as fractional reserve banking, a practice with a storied history extending back centuries. This system permits banks to lend more money than they hold in reserves, essentially conjuring money out of thin air. The Federal Reserve instituted this system, and until 2020, it mandated that banks maintain a 10% reserve. In simple terms, if every customer decided to withdraw all their money simultaneously, the bank would only have 10% of the total deposits on hand.

Analogous to a Ponzi scheme, fractional reserve banking hinges on a steady influx of new funds to remain sustainable. Given that banks are only obligated to have

10% of customer deposits readily available, they are vulnerable to Bank Runs - a phenomenon where a rush of withdrawals exposes a bank's liquidity deficit, leading to its potential collapse. The 1946 film "It's a Wonderful Life," starring James Stewart, offers a vivid depiction of the precarious nature of a bank operating under a fractional reserve system, emphasizing the crucial roles of trust and community support. However, the happy resolution in that movie would unlikely be the probable outcome of present-day bank runs. At present, the US is witnessing a rising tide of bank failures, which, at the time of writing, have already surpassed the total amount of FDIC bailouts from the 2008 crisis.

Considering the 2008 financial crisis and the collapses of institutions like Silicon Valley Bank, Signature Bank, Silvergate Bank, Credit Suisse, First Republic, and others, it's evident that trust in modern banking institutions is far from guaranteed. Today's banks grapple with a host of issues that undermine their reliability. These include predatory lending practices, discriminatory behaviors, connections to money laundering, drug trafficking, and child exploitation, irresponsible risk-taking in mortgage and commercial real estate markets, and vulnerability to manipulation by Federal Reserve interest rate adjustments - the list is extensive and distressing.

Compounding these issues, emergency measures enacted during the COVID-19 crisis in 2020 have further destabilized the banking system. Banks were previously required to maintain a 10% reserve, but this requirement was slashed to zero in response to the pandemic. Yes, that's correct, zero. This reduction has created a precarious situation where the stability of the entire banking system hangs in the balance.

I'm safe because my deposits are FDIC insured, right?

Grasping the fact that banks operate with no reserve requirement at all, you might understandably question the safety of your deposits. The supposed safety net of FDIC insurance is not as robust as many believe and, like any insurance, it can fail.

Let's debunk five significant misconceptions about FDIC insurance:

- FDIC safeguards your deposits - While it's true that FDIC is backed by the full faith and credit of the US government, the safety of your deposits is uncertain, given the government's ballooning debt. As of this book's writing, FDIC's insurance reserve account holds about 0.6% of the total amount of bank deposits. If another major bank collapses, the entire fund is exhausted. Furthermore, at the time of writing, the US Government is perilously close to a default on its debt as it once again approaches the debt ceiling.
- FDIC halts bank runs - The insurance provided by FDIC actually creates a moral hazard, encouraging banks to take on more risks. We've witnessed this play out in the first five months of 2023.
- FDIC ensures financial stability - In reality, the agency might contribute to instability by encouraging moral hazard and rescuing failing banks.
- FDIC acts as an impartial regulator - As a government body, the FDIC has its own agenda and interests, which may not align with the banks it regulates or the depositors it pledges to protect.

- FDIC insurance is cost-free - Banks pay premiums which are indirectly passed on to customers through lower interest rates and higher fees. With FDIC's reserves nearly depleted by 2023's bank failures, these additional fees could drive customers to relocate their money-to-money market funds and other alternative assets, accelerating the pace of bank runs.

Americans lose confidence in bank deposit safety

Recent bank failures in the U.S. have triggered significant worry amongst Americans regarding the safety of their deposits, with about half expressing concern, according to a Gallup poll. This anxiety is particularly elevated among Republicans, independents, and individuals without a college degree. Interestingly, the current unease mirrors sentiments observed during the 2008 financial crisis. In a startling development, the Federal Deposit Insurance Corporation (FDIC) that insures deposits up to $250,000 has exhausted most of its funds due to the number of recent bank failures.

In an attempt to replenish its coffers, the FDIC has had to resort to levying special assessments on larger banks. This situation has elevated the level of concern among the general populace about the reliability of FDIC insurance. In such uncertain economic times, it seems that the public's concern over the safety of their bank deposits is indeed valid and not misplaced.

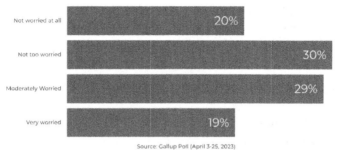

Almost Half of Americans Worry About Safety of Money in Banks

Not worried at all	20%
Not too worried	30%
Moderately Worried	29%
Very worried	19%

Source: Gallup Poll (April 3-25, 2023)

The US Dollar is quickly losing its global reserve currency status

The U.S. Dollar, currently in its 103rd year as the global reserve currency, has outlasted the usual average lifespan for such a status. However, signs indicate that its reign may be waning. Over the past few decades, the proportion of the U.S. dollar as a global reserve currency has seen a significant decrease. Falling from a robust 74% in 1980, it now accounts for just 58% of the global reserve. This downward trajectory is picking up steam and is in near term jeopardy.

The Decline of the US Dollar as Global Reserve Currency

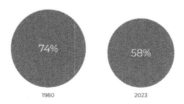

74%
1980

58%
2023

The US dollar has dropped from 74% to 58% of the global reserve currency over the past 40 years.

Source: International Monetary Fund

The rise of the BRICs

The coalition of Brazil, Russia, India, China, and South Africa, known as the BRICs, is emerging as a significant force on the global landscape, challenging the longstanding dominance of the U.S. and the Western world. As of 2023, their combined contribution to the global GDP stands at a robust 31.5%, symbolizing their escalating economic might. The growing appeal of this powerhouse alliance is demonstrated by the 13 nations currently in the pipeline for membership, indicating an expanding influence.

This economic shift extends beyond GDP growth, with the BRICs actively questioning the U.S. Dollar's unassailable position as the global reserve currency. As part of this pivot, an alliance of 24 nations, including the BRICs, is strategizing to reduce their reliance on the dollar, further challenging Western economic dominance.

Current projections suggest that by 2030, the BRICs, along with the developing economies, will surpass the combined GDP of the Western nations. Their rise is not limited to economic dimensions but extends to other vital sectors including technology, military, and geopolitical influence. This indicates a significant repositioning of power dynamics in the global order, emphasizing the evolving strength of the BRICs in contrast to the Western world.

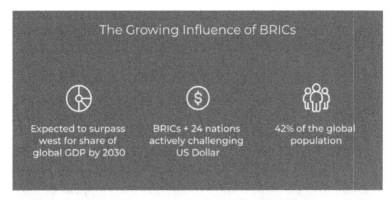

The Growing Influence of BRICs

Expected to surpass west for share of global GDP by 2030

BRICs + 24 nations actively challenging US Dollar

42% of the global population

Poised to take over the west by many key metrics within the decade

*Source World Bank

Bank runs and a squeeze on the money supply

In 2022, U.S. banks had a staggering $18.0 trillion in deposits. However, the first four months of 2023 witnessed a drastic plunge in these deposits, down to $17.2 trillion - a reduction of over $800 billion. This has triggered a financial predicament commonly referred to as a "run on the banks," where many customers withdraw their deposits simultaneously due to fears of the bank's solvency.

Banks don't merely stockpile deposits; they use them to finance various investments. However, considering rising interest rates, many depositors are seeking more lucrative alternatives, such as buying U.S. government bonds. This shift forces banks to sell their investments, often at a loss, to fulfill the sudden surge in withdrawal requests, exacerbating their financial instability.

For instance, Silicon Valley Bank was put in a situation where they had to liquidate their U.S. government bonds at a loss to satisfy withdrawal demands. This unfortunately led to the bank's eventual downfall. This event underlines the current state of financial instability and the ongoing run on the banks in the U.S. financial sector.

As you can see in the graph below there's been a sharp decrease in the M2 money supply (which includes cash, checking deposits, and easily convertible near money) by an enormous $2.9 trillion. The last time we saw such a contraction was during the Great Depression in the 1930s. This alarming trend isn't limited to the U.S. alone; it's a global issue, impacting Europe, Asia, and the Middle East.

This massive drop is largely due to current instability in the financial sector, with banks witnessing a large withdrawal of deposits. When people pull their money out of banks, it shrinks the money supply, which can lead to economic uncertainty. Simply put, less money in circulation can spell trouble, causing economic turbulence and making financial experts quite anxious.

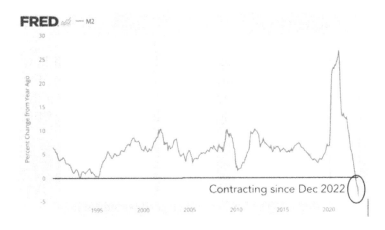

To recap:

- The dollar, previously backed by gold, is now backed only by government IOUs—debts that taxpayers must repay, with interest, to the Federal Reserve. It's worth noting that the Federal Reserve is a consortium of private banks that is neither federal nor maintains reserves.

- The repayment of principal and interest is enforced by armed IRS agents, funded by taxpayers.
- During the COVID crisis, banks' reserve requirement—a provision to hold 10% of customer deposits—was reduced to 0%.
- The FDIC insurance fund maintains reserves amounting to just 0.6% of customer deposits, insufficient to weather another large bank failure.
- Almost half of Americans don't think their bank account is safe.
- The Dollar is rapidly losing its global reserve currency status.
- The BRICs will overtake the west in GDP by 2030.
- People are pulling their money out of banks at record levels.

Keeping this in mind, let's take a high-level view of how the US Dollar standard compares to historical fiat currencies that have failed, examining them through the lens of Mike Hewitt's top reasons for the collapse of fiat currency:

Reasons for Fiat Failure	US Dollar Examples
1. Inflation	The US has experienced periods of high inflation, such as the 1970s, and the US printed 40% of the dollars ever in existence as part of the 2020 COVID response
2. Loss of confidence	The dollar's status as the world's reserve currency is being challenged by Brazil, Russia, India, China, and Saudi Arabia who are seeking to reduce their reliance on the dollar.

3. Debt overload	The US national debt has surpassed $31 trillion, raising concerns about the long-term sustainability of the country's fiscal position. The US is less than one month away from defaulting on its debt.
4. Economic mismanagement	Critics argue that the Federal Reserve's monetary policies, including low interest rates and quantitative easing, contribute to boom-bust cycles and exacerbate wealth inequality.
5. Currency competition	Cryptocurrencies like Bitcoin are gaining popularity as alternatives to fiat currencies, potentially undermining the dollar's dominance. BRIC nations are seeking to reduce their reliance on the dollar There has been a resurgence of interest in gold and silver.
6. Political turmoil	The United States is currently on the brink of World War III supporting Ukraine against Russia and Taiwan against China. Internally, the country is at a point of civil unrest.
7. Technological changes	The rise of digital currencies, including central bank digital currencies (CBDCs), could disrupt the traditional financial system and the role of the US dollar.

Looking at the broader context, it's apparent that fiat currencies are predisposed to failure. Upon a detailed examination, the US Dollar seems to be teetering on the edge of a precipice, having severed its ties with the gold standard, operating in a fractional reserve-free environment, and offering only a thin safety net of FDIC insurance.

When juxtaposing the Dollar with other fiat currencies that have collapsed, its eventual downfall seems almost inevitable. Add to this the influence of global entities such as the UN, WEF, World Bank, IMF, and BIS, which seem determined to hasten the demise of fiat currencies and pave the way for a new era of CBDCs, and the urgency for collective response becomes glaringly obvious.

This is the moment for us to band together, forsake the sinking ship of fiat currencies, and embrace self-custodial alternatives like cryptocurrency, gold, and silver. We must extricate ourselves from the relentless cycle of fiat failure while concurrently fending off the looming threat of CBDC domination. The stakes have never been higher, and the call for decisive action has never been louder. Our financial freedom hangs in the balance.

The remainder of this book will delve into specific strategies for exiting the fiat world and sidestepping the potential tyranny of CBDCs. We'll kickstart our exploration with the universe of cryptocurrencies. Despite the vastness of the topic, I've endeavored to streamline the content and guide you directly towards cryptocurrencies that can effectively function as alternatives to fiat or CBDC. We'll also probe into the realms of self-custody gold and silver, equipping you with a variety of options as we brace ourselves for imminent economic and political turbulence.

7 Key Takeaways from Chapter 5:

- Throughout history, all fiat currencies have eventually failed, with examples spanning from ancient Rome to modern-day Zimbabwe.
- The United States, despite its economic prowess, is not immune to the risks of fiat currency collapse and is currently demonstrating multiple indicators of imminent collapse.
- El Salvador's experiment with Bitcoin as legal tender offers insight into a potential future where

cryptocurrencies may play a significant role in national economies.

- The separation of money and government could provide an opportunity to break the cycle of fiat currency failure caused by government corruption and mismanagement.
- Cryptocurrencies, like Bitcoin, offer potential benefits such as increased financial inclusion, reduced reliance on remittances, and attracting foreign investment.
- Understanding the risks and potential of cryptocurrencies is crucial for navigating the future of global finance and avoiding the pitfalls that have plagued fiat currencies.
- The globalist organizations (UN, WEF, World Bank, IMF, BIS) want to replace fiat with something worse – CBDC. Self-custody crypto, gold, silver is the way to stop this tyranny.

Artwork:

"The root problem with conventional currency is all the trust that's required to make it work. The central bank must be trusted not to debase the currency, but the history of fiat currencies is full of breaches of that trust."
- Satoshi Nakamoto

In digital realms, a tale unfolds,
Of currencies that break the molds,
Facing trials and bitter strife,
Crypto pioneers change our life.

Through government's unyielding grip,
The dream of freedom shall not slip,
For in this revolution, we stand,
With cryptocurrencies, hand in hand.

Chapter 6 Crypto Revolution: Empowering Financial Freedom in a Turbulent World

In these critical times, we can't ignore the glaring reality: fiat currencies are on the precipice of failure, and the US dollar is no exception. The stage is set for a global power grab, as elites aim to replace these failing systems with Central Bank Digital Currencies (CBDCs) — a move that could usher in unprecedented control and tyranny. However, there is still light at the end of the tunnel. The rest of this book will illuminate practical, effective solutions for reclaiming our financial futures. Time is of the essence; with FedNow's implementation in July 2023, the sands in our hourglass are quickly dwindling, making prompt action vital.

In this chapter, we'll navigate the revolutionary realm of cryptocurrency, a game-changing monetary system that defies the historical pitfalls of government-backed fiat currencies. Amidst the cacophony of thousands of cryptos, we'll identify a handpicked selection that could serve as robust alternatives to both fiat and CBDCs. Additionally, we'll underscore the importance of self-custody, spotlighting the risks associated with third-party exchanges and the ongoing fight against the US government's attempts to monopolize money. This chapter will lay the groundwork for Chapter 10, which provides a detailed guide on procuring and securely storing the right cryptocurrencies within a quarter of an hour, plus insights on how to incorporate crypto into your everyday life.

My journey with crypto started in 2012, and it has drastically reshaped my understanding of finance, economics, and liberty. I relocated to New Hampshire in 2009 as part of the Free State Project (FSP), a movement mobilizing 20,000 individuals to preserve the state's "Live Free or Die" ethos and uphold liberty in our lifetimes. New Hampshire boasts one of the highest per capita usage rates of crypto globally. I've utilized crypto in various ways, from fundraising for political campaigns and activism to going all in on crypto in 2019 when I realized fiat's inevitable collapse. In New Hampshire, I'm not alone—several individuals exclusively rely on crypto for their livelihoods (some for even longer than I have). This chapter distills not only my research but also my decade-long personal experiences, and the shared experiences of those who have been pioneering the escape from the failing world of fiat.

Why This Chapter Matters

Understanding the workings of cryptocurrency and its advantages within the financial landscape enables us to leverage this potent technology effectively. Gaining knowledge on how to procure self-custody cryptocurrencies judiciously and operate them securely offers us alternatives to the crumbling world of fiat currencies. Recognizing the challenges cryptocurrencies may encounter from governmental interference and exchange failures underscores the significance of self-custody.

This awareness provides us with the tools to manage our financial futures and establish safeguards against growing instability. Engaging in the cryptocurrency revolution promotes self-reliance, robustness, and optimism for a fairer monetary system.

What is crypto?

There are thousands of cryptocurrencies and tokens with a huge array of different features and capabilities. My goal isn't to cover the broad range of crypto. My goal is to focus only on cryptocurrencies that can be used as a superior form of money to either fiat currency or CBDC.

Imagine a world where you can send and receive money instantly, without the need for banks, and without the worry of counterfeit bills or identity theft. That's the vision behind cryptocurrency, and Bitcoin, its most well-known example.

In simple terms, Bitcoin is digital money. It exists entirely online, and it allows you to buy goods and services or even send money to your friends and family just like you would with traditional cash. What sets it apart, though, is that it is not controlled by any government or institution. This means that it offers more privacy and freedom than traditional currencies.

To understand how Bitcoin works, think of it as a giant, public ledger. This ledger keeps a record of all transactions made with Bitcoin, and it is maintained by a network of computers all over the world. These computers use complex mathematical problems to verify and secure the transactions. Once a transaction is verified, it is added to the ledger, and it cannot be altered or deleted. This ensures that no one can cheat the system or create fake Bitcoins.

One of the most revolutionary aspects of Bitcoin is the technology behind it, called blockchain. A blockchain is a series of digital "blocks" that contain transaction data. Each block is connected to the one before it and the one after it, creating a chain. This chain is incredibly secure because if anyone tried to alter a block, they would need to change every block that comes after it, which is practically impossible.

So why has Bitcoin become so popular? There are a few reasons. First, it offers a level of privacy and security that traditional banks and payment systems cannot match. Since it is not controlled by any single authority, it is less likely to be manipulated or affected by government policies. Additionally, the transaction fees for Bitcoin are generally lower than those of traditional banking systems. Also, there is a fixed supply of Bitcoin. There will only ever be 21 million Bitcoin. As we have seen with the failure of fiat currencies, governments tend to print massive amounts of money leading to inflation. Even gold and silver have been debased by mixing inferior metals to give the illusion that there is more supply than actually exists.. With Bitcoin that isn't possible. The supply is capped at 21 million.

Crypto as a monetary revolution

Bitcoin is truly peer-to-peer cash for the world. Anyone on planet Earth can send and receive money without the need for corrupt and inefficient banks and government middlemen adding fees, inflating the currency, censoring the money, and creating barriers. This is truly revolutionary and something that has never been possible.

Not only is Bitcoin better at handling the kinds of transactions the fiat banking system handles, but the technology also offers the ability to do things that have never been done with traditional fiat money. The current fiat system is both slow and expense. For example, did you know that when you buy something at a store with your credit card or debit card the merchant pays a fee (typically $0.30 plus 2.9% of the amount of the transaction)? This means that it isn't economically viable for businesses to make money on small dollar transactions using credit or debit cards. On top of the fees, the merchant usually must wait 1-3 days before they receive the funds from your credit card.

With Bitcoin (certain versions of it) it is possible to send and receive money for a fraction of a penny. The transaction is completely settled within minutes. A few years ago, the Federal Reserve had a technical outage and banks were unable to send money to one another. I used that as an opportunity to send a bunch of people $.01 of a cryptocurrency called Ravencoin. Why did I do this? Because I could. I wanted to demonstrate that I could send an amount of money as small as one penny anywhere in the world nearly instantly and at a cost in the hundredths of a penny while at the same time the largest central bank in the world was offline. Many took me up on the offer, and I sent $0.01 worth of RVN to people in South Korea, the UK, South America, and several other countries.

You might be thinking "Nice trick, but what is the real-world use of that?" I will tell you. These micropayments open up a world of completely new business models. All the major big tech platforms like Facebook, Instagram, and Twitter (although Twitter is starting to evolve) operate using advertising models. While these companies claim to be free to users, you, more specifically your data, are the product that they are selling to advertisers. In a world with crypto micropayments, instead of seeing targeted ads (and biased results) on Google, you could instead pay a fraction of a penny every time you do a search – yielding better, unbiased results while preserving your data and privacy. Or imagine instead of paying to rent a movie, you only pay for what you watch. Maybe you rent a movie and 10 minutes in realize it's a stinker. With micropayments you could pay for just what you watch.

Which are the right coins?

I have mentioned two cryptocurrencies so far, Bitcoin and Ravencoin. If you search around or see celebrities endorsing cryptos, which I advise you to avoid anything in crypto with a celebrity endorsement, you will find there are thousands of cryptocurrencies. I am going cut through all the noise and get you to a handful or so of coins that are worthy of your attention.

The primary focus of this exercise is to find cryptocurrencies that can replace fiat currency as money for daily transactions. The blockchain technology that underlies a crypto like Bitcoin can have many applications. I am going to narrow our search field to only those coins that can be used in the regular buying and selling of goods.

Because crypto is a threat to the government monopoly on money, we need to narrow our search to coins that can't be easily shutdown by governments (either technically or legally). Any coin project that raised money through the sale of its token to the public through what is called an Initial Coin Offering (ICO) is likely an illegal security and is at risk of getting shutdown by the government. The Securities and Exchange Commission (SEC) has been very aggressive in going after these types of companies. I would argue that we need to significantly reform if not get rid of the SEC altogether.

Nevertheless, the reality of the situation is that under current US securities laws, most if not all projects that raised money through these token sales is at risk of getting shut down. In addition, many of these projects that raised money through these token sales turned out to be scams. Take the case of OneCoin, which claimed to be a revolutionary digital currency and turned out to be a $4 billion pyramid scheme. In a statement from the US Attorney's Office for the Southern District of New York, the OneCoin scheme was described as "an old scam with a virtual twist", and the founders were accused of "lying about the success of OneCoin, the amount of investment, and the value of the cryptocurrency". The statement went on to say that "this is one of the largest cryptocurrency frauds ever committed." Ruja Ignatova, the founder of OneCoin is on the FBI's most wanted list and there is a $100,000 reward for information leading to her arrest. As you will learn later, almost all crypto projects that did an ICO probably didn't comply with securities laws and are likely to be deemed illegal by the SEC. You will want to stay away from all of these.

We also want to stay away from crypto projects that are centralized and controlled by a single entity. We will want to ignore any cryptos that are controlled by corporate entities. At the end of the day, a government could seize these entities via a court order, and depending on how the technology works, the project could be halted, or transactions reversed. In addition, if they are centralized from a technology perspective, a small group of developers could take over the project – potentially stealing coins or reversing transactions.

We also want to stay away from proof-of-stake models (POS). Proof-of-stake is touted as a more energy-efficient method for validating transactions on a blockchain, where users put up a "stake" of their cryptocurrency as collateral to ensure honest behavior. These POS systems can lead to centralization and favor the wealthy (the larger the "stake" the more control you have over the system). This approach isn't much different from our current centrally controlled banking system or the proposed CBDC models. One notable failure was the DAO, a decentralized autonomous organization (DAO) that was built on the Ethereum blockchain. It was launched in April 2016 and raised over $150 million in funding from over 11,000 investors. The DAO was designed to be a venture capital fund that would invest in other cryptocurrencies and decentralized applications.

In June 2016, a hacker exploited a vulnerability in the DAO's code and stole over $50 million worth of Ethereum. The hack was the largest theft of cryptocurrency in history at the time. The Ethereum community was divided on how to respond to the hack. Some people argued that the DAO should be hard forked, which would mean rewriting the Ethereum blockchain to reverse the effects of the hack. Others argued that the DAO should not be hard forked, as this would set a precedent for reversing other hacks in the future. In the end, the Ethereum community decided to hard fork the blockchain. The hard fork was successful, and the stolen Ethereum was returned to its rightful owners. However, the hard fork also created two separate versions of the Ethereum blockchain: Ethereum (ETH) and Ethereum Classic (ETC). The ability for transactions to be reversed like this on Ethereum is a big red flag and could be exploited in the future by governments or bad actors. We know that we are facing a huge threat of centralization and need solutions that prevent this.

As with ICOs, it also looks as though the SEC has set its sights on POS projects as well. POS projects that have a centralized organization or large stakeholders are vulnerable to being controlled by either government entities or large stakeholders. I suggest staying away from all these projects as well.

You would be amazed at how many of the crypto projects get removed from the list once you filter for projects that raised money, have a corporate structure, or operate using the POS (proof-of-stake) model for validating transactions.

Now that we know what we don't want, let's discuss what we are looking for. Let's delve into the technical aspects of Bitcoin. Bitcoin is a decentralized digital currency that operates on a peer-to-peer network. It relies on cryptography to secure transactions and control the creation of new units. What sets it apart?

• Censorship resistance: No central authority can dictate who uses Bitcoin or manipulate its value. This ensures a global, borderless financial system where transactions are free from interference.
• Consensus mechanism: Bitcoin uses Proof-of-Work (POW), where miners compete to solve

mathematical puzzles and add new transaction blocks to the blockchain. This fosters decentralization and security.

- Competitive nature: The POW mining process encourages competition, preventing any single entity from controlling the network.

We want projects that are like Bitcoin, and, as we stated above, we want to make sure that we select projects that didn't do an ICO or are controlled by any centralized organization. We are looking for pure open-source protocols that have the design of Bitcoin.

As you learn more about Bitcoin you will learn that there is considerable debate and controversy within the Bitcoin community. The original Bitcoin protocol was modified and there are several competing blockchains that have split off from the original design. I could write a completely separate book on this topic alone; however, I want to focus this book at an introductory level and make you aware of a handful of projects that use the underlying Bitcoin technology that are worthy of your consideration.

Here is a list of projects based on the underlying Bitcoin technology that I believe are worthy of your consideration as suitable alternatives to fiat currency and CBDCs.

Crypto	Primary Purpose	Max Supply	Block Time	Avg.	Key Features
Ravencoin (RVN) 2018	Asset Transfer	21 Billion	1 min	Low	Asset creation, rewards program, messaging
Bitcoin (BTC) 2009	Digital Gold	21 Million	10 min	High	First cryptocurrency, secure, widely adopted
Bitcoin Cash (BCH) 2017	Digital Cash, low fees	21 Million	10 min	Low-Medium	Faster transactions, bigger blocks, lower fees
Litecoin (LTC) 2011	Digital Silver	84 Million	2.5 min	Medium	Faster than Bitcoin, lower fees, widely adopted
Bitcoin SV (BSV) 2018	Scalability, low fees	21 Million	10 min	Low	Massive on-chain scaling, low fees, fast payments

Ravencoin (RVN): Launched in 2018, Ravencoin is designed for transferring assets like tokens between users. These tokens can be used to trade anything (real estate, wine, stocks, bonds, gold, silver, NFTs, etc.).

Aside: NFTs, or Non-Fungible Tokens, are the digital art world's latest darlings. But what exactly are they?
Imagine owning a one-of-a-kind piece of artwork — a distinct, irreplaceable item with its own unique value. That's what an NFT is, but in the digital realm. Unlike cryptocurrencies like Bitcoin or Ravencoin, which are fungible and can be exchanged on a like-for-like basis,

NFTs are unique. Each one has its own specific information, value, and digital signature.

But how does this work in the digital world, where everything can be copied? The magic lies in the blockchain technology that underpins NFTs. The same technology that ensures the security of cryptocurrencies also verifies the authenticity and ownership of these digital assets.

When you purchase an NFT, you're buying a digital certificate of ownership that's secured on the blockchain. This certificate includes unique information about the digital asset — who made it, who owns it, and any previous transactions. It's like having a digital authenticity certificate that's impossible to forge.

NFTs can represent anything digital — artwork, music, tweets, virtual real estate, and even virtual pets. When you buy an NFT, you're buying the "original" version of these digital assets. While anyone can view or download a digital image or song, only the owner of the NFT has the "official" version.

Ravencoin offers unique features like asset creation, rewards programs, and messaging systems. RVN has a maximum supply of 21 billion coins, a block time of 1 minute, and generally low transaction fees. In a previous chapter we talked about the Regulated Liability Network (RLN) which is basically a centralized framework that would allow governments and 3rd parties to monitor, regulate, and censor not only CBDC but digital assets as well. Ravencoin is essentially the opposite of this. With Ravencoin, you can tokenize anything (stocks, bonds, cars, homes, art) and trade these tokens anywhere in the world without any 3rd party and it is nearly instant and costs a fraction of a penny. I have traded everything from wine to silver to artwork using Ravencoin and have even helped my kids digitize and sell their artwork through Ravencoin. Ravencoin can serve as money as well as a platform for trading digital assets of all sizes and values.

Bitcoin (BTC): Created in 2009, Bitcoin is often referred to as digital gold. It is widely adopted, secure, and has a limited supply of 21 million coins. With a block time of 10 minutes, BTC's transaction fees are relatively high compared to other cryptocurrencies. Around 2017, the BTC community decided to intentionally limit what is called the base layer of BTC to 7 transactions per second. Because of this, BTC is primarily seen as digital gold as opposed to a cryptocurrency that can be used for daily transactions. There is an experiment called Lightning Network that was built on top of BTC to handle these types of transactions; however, there are claims that this system is centralized and doesn't solve the problem of BTC's underlying small block/limited transaction capacity. This was recently demonstrated when a group of people started launching NFTs on BTC. This increased demand for the network and dramatically increased the cost and time to process transactions for both the base layer of BTC and Lightning Network.

Bitcoin Cash (BCH): If you've spent some time exploring the world of cryptocurrencies, you've probably come across the term 'fork.' It's a term borrowed from software development, and it describes a situation where a single project splits into two different paths. In the world of cryptocurrencies, a fork happens when there's a significant change or disagreement about the rules governing the blockchain.

Let's imagine the blockchain as a busy highway. All the cars (transactions) follow the same set of rules

143

(protocol), traveling smoothly. However, suppose a group of drivers decides they want to change some of these rules — maybe they want to drive faster or take a different route. In that case, they can choose to take a different exit and form a new highway. This is akin to what happens in a blockchain fork.

Bitcoin Cash is a prime example of a fork. Born out of a disagreement in the Bitcoin community about how to handle scaling issues, Bitcoin Cash took a different path (a 'fork' in the road, if you will) in 2017. The creators of Bitcoin Cash wanted a version of Bitcoin that was more practical for everyday transactions — like buying coffee or paying for groceries.

To make this possible, they increased Bitcoin's 'block size.' Think of each block as a car on our imaginary highway. By making the cars bigger, they could hold more passengers (transactions), which theoretically would make the entire system faster and more efficient.

As a result, Bitcoin Cash has a larger block size than Bitcoin (up to 32MB compared to Bitcoin's 1MB), allowing it to process more transactions per block. This is intended to result in faster transaction times and lower fees, making it more practical for everyday use.

I've personally found Bitcoin Cash to be a valuable tool for everyday transactions.

Litecoin (LTC): Litecoin, introduced to the digital world in 2011, was envisioned as a 'lite' version of Bitcoin. It was designed by Charlie Lee, a Google engineer at the time, who sought to create a cryptocurrency that could complement Bitcoin, much like silver complements gold in the traditional financial world. This is why Litecoin is often referred to as the "silver" to Bitcoin's "gold."

Litecoin bears some similarities to Bitcoin. Both are decentralized, meaning they operate without a central authority, and both provide a transparent transaction history accessible to anyone, ensuring accountability and trustworthiness. Like Bitcoin, Litecoin also has a cap on the number of coins that can ever exist — 84 million, precisely four times as many as Bitcoin's maximum supply.

However, there are several distinguishing features that make Litecoin stand out. Firstly, Litecoin's block generation time — the time it takes to confirm a new block of transactions on the network — is about 2.5 minutes, compared to Bitcoin's 10 minutes. This faster speed means that transactions can be confirmed more quickly, which can be particularly useful for time-sensitive purchases.

Secondly, Litecoin uses a different hashing algorithm called Scrypt, while Bitcoin uses SHA-256. Without getting too technical, these algorithms are like the engines that keep the Litecoin and Bitcoin networks running. Scrypt was chosen for Litecoin because it's generally considered to be more accessible to new miners, requiring less computational power and energy than SHA-256.

When it comes to transaction fees, Litecoin typically has lower costs than Bitcoin, making it a potentially more appealing choice for smaller, everyday transactions. Moreover, it's widely accepted by many merchants and is readily available for trading on most cryptocurrency exchanges.

To sum it up, Litecoin was designed to offer a more accessible and practical alternative to Bitcoin, particularly for smaller, everyday transactions. Its faster block generation time and lower transaction fees are part of its appeal.

Bitcoin SV (BSV): BSV is a version of Bitcoin that was created in 2018. It comes from another version called Bitcoin Cash, which itself comes from the original Bitcoin. BSV aims to follow the original idea of Bitcoin, as suggested by its creator, 'Satoshi Nakamoto'.

The main goal of BSV is to be faster, more efficient, and have low fees, making it useful for everyday transactions.
BSV can handle up to 50,000 transactions per second and has plans to increase that to over 1 million transactions per second. This is a big improvement compared to the original Bitcoin's 7 transactions per second. Thanks to its larger capacity, BSV can be used for small payments, digital contracts, and creating tokens.

However, BSV has caused a lot of debate. The main person behind the controversy, Craig Wright, claims to be Satoshi Nakamoto, the creator of Bitcoin which, in my opinion after spending hundreds of hours reading his papers and watching his videos seems very plausible. I have personally used BSV to buy gift cards and have also experienced the micropayment aspect of BSV through a service called Twetch. Twetch is a social network (like Twitter) without ads. You pay pennies to post content and to like and share other people's content. They also have a marketplace for NFTs. They have truly demonstrated that micropayments can work.

Environmental Impact of Bitcoin: A Net Improvement

The creation of Bitcoin has revolutionized the financial world, offering a way to reduce corruption and increase energy efficiency compared to the traditional banking system. However, many people remain unaware of the full scope of these benefits. This section will explore the environmental impact of Bitcoin and argue that its advantages far outweigh its drawbacks.

Firstly, let's compare the energy usage of the traditional banking system with that of Bitcoin. The table below demonstrates that Bitcoin consumes far less energy overall:

System	Energy Consumption
Traditional Banking	Branches (heating, cooling, lighting), ATMs (electricity), Data Centers (servers, cooling), Transportation (cash transport, employee commuting), Paper production (statements, marketing materials) deforestation
Bitcoin	Mining (hardware, electricity), Network (node operation), Transactions (validation, broadcasting)

While Bitcoin mining has been criticized for its energy consumption, it's crucial to consider the extensive energy usage of the entire traditional banking system. This includes energy costs for branches, ATMs, data centers, transportation, and paper production.

Is Proof-of-Stake a more energy efficient alternative?

Proof of Stake (POS) is a consensus mechanism used in certain blockchain networks. Consensus mechanisms are essentially the rules that determine how transactions are validated and added to the blockchain. Bitcoin, for instance, uses a consensus mechanism known as Proof of Work (PoW).

In Proof of Work, miners compete against each other using computational power to solve complex mathematical problems. The first one to solve the problem gets to add a new block to the blockchain and is rewarded with some Bitcoin. However, this process consumes a lot of energy, which has raised environmental concerns.

This is where Proof of Stake comes in as an alternative. Instead of miners competing with computational power, validators are chosen to create new blocks based on the amount of cryptocurrency they hold and are willing to "stake" or temporarily lock up as collateral. In other words, the more coins you're willing to stake, the higher your chances of being chosen to validate transactions and add a new block to the blockchain. This method significantly reduces the amount of energy required.

Despite its advantages, it's important to recognize that Proof of Stake isn't a silver bullet solution. It doesn't necessarily solve problems like centralization or corruption. In fact, one could argue that it potentially exacerbates the issue of centralization since those with more coins have a higher chance of being chosen as validators, leading to a situation where the rich get richer.

Moreover, by focusing on energy efficiency, POS doesn't directly confront the deeper issues that have plagued traditional financial systems, like corruption, lack of transparency, and manipulation by third parties. Therefore, it's not entirely accurate to call it a complete upgrade from the current financial system. It might be more fitting to consider it, as some do, as a "Federal Reserve 2.0," with its own set of strengths and limitations.

Bitcoin's primary invention is to break the boom/bust cycle of failed fiat currencies, bring integrity to peer-to-peer commerce, and empower individual freedom across the globe. The environmental impact of Bitcoin, when compared to the current system, is a significant net improvement.

As 2024 Democratic Presidential Candidate Robert F. Kennedy, Jr. states, "Yes, energy use is a concern (though somewhat overstated), but bitcoin mining uses about the same as video games and no one is calling for a ban on those. The environmental argument is a selective pretext to suppress anything that threatens elite power structures."

Privacy coins

In the digital age where every action can leave a footprint, privacy has become a rare commodity, and this is especially true in the world of cryptocurrencies. While Bitcoin transactions are pseudonymous (meaning they are not directly linked to real-world identities), they are not completely private. All Bitcoin transactions are recorded on a public ledger, or blockchain, which is accessible to anyone who wants to view it. This means that if your Bitcoin address can be linked to your real-world identity, your transactions can, in principle, be traced back to you.

This is where privacy coins like Monero and Zcash come into play. These cryptocurrencies are designed with a strong emphasis on privacy and anonymity.

Unlike Bitcoin, they employ advanced cryptographic techniques to obscure the details of their transactions.

Take Monero, for example. It uses something called ring signatures to shuffle a user's public keys with others, making it nearly impossible to identify a specific user's signature. It also uses stealth addresses, which are one-time addresses created for each transaction on behalf of the recipient. This means that different payments sent to the same recipient cannot be linked.

Zcash, on the other hand, uses a different technology called zk-SNARKs, or "zero-knowledge proofs". This allows the network to validate transactions without revealing any information about the sender, recipient, or the amount transacted.

While privacy coins offer enhanced anonymity, it's important to note that this feature can be a double-edged sword. On the one hand, they can provide a crucial layer of protection for individuals living under oppressive regimes or anyone who values their financial privacy. On the other hand, they can also be misused for illicit activities.

As such, if the governments tighten regulations on cryptocurrency or increase censorship, holding a certain proportion of your portfolio in privacy coins could be a strategic move.

The Failure of Centralized Exchanges and the Importance of Self-custody

Now that you know what types of cryptocurrencies you should consider buying, we will delve into how to buy them, and, more importantly, how to store them.

"Not your keys, not your crypto" is a phrase used to remind people that if they don't have control over the private keys for their cryptocurrency, they don't truly own it. Think of private keys like the keys to a safe. If you have the keys, you can access what's inside, but if someone else has them, they have control over your valuables.

In the context of cryptocurrency, many people store their coins on exchanges or online wallets. While this may be convenient, it also means that the company running the exchange or wallet holds the private keys, and they have control over your crypto. If the company gets hacked, goes out of business, or experiences technical issues, you could lose access to your cryptocurrency.

To truly own and control your cryptocurrency, it's important to hold your private keys in a secure wallet that only you can access, such as a hardware wallet or a well-protected software wallet. This way, you ensure that you're the only one with the "keys" to your crypto "safe," giving you complete control and ownership.

Having been immersed in the world of crypto for over a decade, I cannot stress enough the importance of never leaving your cryptocurrencies on exchanges. Unfortunately, I've witnessed far too many individuals lose some or even all their crypto assets due to this oversight. Time and time again, I urge people to move their coins off exchanges to ensure their safety.

It's disheartening to see individuals embracing the decentralized nature of cryptocurrencies as an alternative to our flawed traditional monetary system, only to lose everything because they placed their trust in a centralized third-party for storage. The hard truth is that no exchange is completely secure; history has shown us that even the largest and most reputable platforms can fall prey to hacks or other forms of failure.

So, if you're serious about safeguarding your crypto investments and embracing the ethos of decentralization, it's crucial to take personal responsibility for the storage and security of your digital assets. By doing so, you'll not only protect your hard-earned crypto but also uphold the principles that make this financial revolution so promising.

Self-custody is like wearing a bulletproof vest in a high-stakes poker game. It means holding the private keys to your crypto assets, giving you full control and responsibility for their safekeeping. In contrast, custody on an exchange or with a third party means they hold the keys, leaving your assets exposed to risks like regulatory crackdowns, hacking, and government seizure.

With billions of dollars lost due to exchange failures, it's crucial to understand why self-custody is essential. I will highlight just 3 of the more colorful crypto exchange collapses (although there are new stories to tell almost every week). In Chapter 10, I will give you a short cut to buying crypto that doesn't involve using an exchange at all. Depending on the amount of crypto you purchase, you might still need to use an exchange, but if you do, withdraw all your coins immediately after making the purchase.

I hope that after you hear about the failure of these 3 crypto exchanges, you will heed my advice and use them only to acquire crypto and never to hold your crypto.

FTX: The Rise and Fall of a Crypto Behemoth

FTX was a cryptocurrency exchange and crypto hedge fund that was founded in 2019 by Sam Bankman-Fried and Gary Wang. The exchange was headquartered in the Bahamas and incorporated in Antigua and Barbuda. FTX was one of the largest cryptocurrency exchanges by volume, and at its peak in July 2021, had over one million users. The exchange offered a variety of trading products that essentially allowed their customers to gamble using leverage. Leverage in the context of a crypto exchange like FTX refers to borrowing funds to amplify your trading position, allowing you to potentially increase your profits (or losses) without needing to invest more of your own money. For example, using 10x leverage on a $100 investment would give you the buying power of $1,000, magnifying the outcome of your trade by 10 times.

In November 2022, FTX filed for bankruptcy after facing a liquidity crisis. The exchange's collapse shook the volatile crypto market, which lost billions at the time, falling below a $1 trillion valuation. FTX was known for its flashy celebrity endorsements from Tom Brady to Larry David (remember what I said about celebrity endorsements?) The founder has been charged with 13 criminal counts including securities fraud, money laundering, and campaign finance violations. Bankman-Fried has been accused of paying a $40 million bribe to Chinese officials (to unfreeze accounts) and contributed over $70 million to election campaigns (mostly Democrats and liberal-leaning groups).

The drama of the story is being encapsulated by Michael Lewis, author of "The Big Short" in a new book and likely movie/TV series. Lewis stated, "The FTX story is a tale of ambition, greed, and the dark side of the crypto industry." The ongoing lawsuit, including bribery charges, adds fuel to the fire as FTX's legacy unravels.

The collapse of FTX devastated many. Here are some quotes from people destroyed by FTX:

- "I lost everything. I had my life savings invested in FTX, and now it's all gone. I don't know what I'm going to do."

- "I'm so angry. I trusted FTX, and they let me down. I'm going to have to start over from scratch."

- "I'm devastated. I lost my retirement savings, and I don't know how I'm going to pay my bills."

- "I'm scared. I don't know how I'm going to support my family."

- "I'm heartbroken. I lost my dream of financial freedom."

Mt. Gox: The Titanic of Crypto Exchanges

Founded in 2010, Mt. Gox was once the world's largest Bitcoin exchange, handling over 70% of all transactions. However, in 2014, Mt. Gox collapsed, losing 850,000 Bitcoins, leaving its customers devastated. The US government stepped in, but the road to recovery has been a long and arduous one for the affected users. In 2022, the trustee for Mt, Gox announced that they had recovered 141,886 bitcoins. These Bitcoins were sold at auction and the proceeds distributed to the creditors (note: 8 years after the initial collapse!)

Mt. Gox has become the poster child for exchange failures, with documentaries made to chronicle its catastrophic downfall. As reported by Investopedia, "The Mt. Gox scandal remains a black mark on the history of Bitcoin and a cautionary tale for investors about the importance of self-custody."

154

Here are some quotes from people directly impacted by the Mt. Gox collapse.

- "I had 311 BTC on Mt. Gox. It represented 95% of my net worth. It's a massive loss for me, and I'm devastated. I don't know what I'm going to do." - User on Reddit
- "I had 12 BTC in my Mt. Gox account. It was my entire Bitcoin holding. I'm upset and sad, but I'm not sure if I'm angrier at Mt. Gox or myself for not keeping my coins in a more secure place." - User on Bitcointalk forum
- "I lost 5 BTC. It's not as much as others, but it still hurts. I was planning on using it to pay off some student loans. Now I have to start over." - User on Twitter
- "I had 50 BTC on Mt. Gox. I can't believe this is happening. I've been in Bitcoin since the beginning, and this is a major setback for me and the community. We need to learn from this and make sure it doesn't happen again." - User on Reddit

- "I lost 2 BTC on Mt. Gox. I'm a college student, and that was a lot of money for me. I feel like I've been robbed, and there's nothing I can do about it." - User on Bitcointalk forum

QuadrigaCX: A Cold Wallet and a Mysterious Death

Let's take a step back and delve into the intriguing saga of QuadrigaCX, a story that would seem more at home in a Hollywood movie script than in the world of crypto exchanges. Picture this: QuadrigaCX, once the crowning glory of Canada's cryptocurrency scene, finds itself thrust into turmoil in the wake of a shocking twist.

In 2018, QuadrigaCX's enigmatic founder, Gerald Cotten, undertakes a philanthropic trip to India. While there, he tragically passes away due to complications from Crohn's disease, leaving the exchange and its customers in a state of utter disarray. Why? Cotten, it turns out, was the sole custodian of the exchange's cold wallets, which contained a staggering $190 million worth of customers' cryptocurrency. His sudden demise meant that he took the only known access to those funds with him to the grave.

The crypto world was left shell-shocked, and customers found themselves locked out of their accounts, unable to access their investments. But as the dust settled, suspicion began to swirl around the peculiar circumstances of Cotten's death and the strange setup of the exchange's security measures. Was it truly possible that Cotten, a veteran in the crypto space, would leave such a massive amount of digital wealth at the mercy of a single point of failure?

These questions began to feed rumors of foul play and whispers of an elaborate exit scam. Independent researchers even claimed that they found no evidence of the exchange's cold wallets. Meanwhile, the graveyard silence from QuadrigaCX only served to stoke the flames of speculation.

Netflix's documentary, "Dead Man's Switch: A Crypto Mystery," delves into the bizarre circumstances surrounding Cotten's death and the fallout for QuadrigaCX's customers. As Cointelegraph reports, "The QuadrigaCX scandal serves as a chilling reminder of the importance of self-custody and the dangers of centralized control in the crypto world."

You can hear in their own words how some of the victims were impacted by the collapse of QuadrigaCX.

- "I had $10,000 worth of cryptocurrency on QuadrigaCX. Now it's all gone, and I'm left wondering how something like this could happen. It's a painful lesson to learn." - User on Reddit
- "I lost 8.5 BTC on QuadrigaCX. I can't believe this is happening. It feels like a bad dream. I wish I had taken more precautions and not kept all my crypto in one place." - User on Twitter
- "I'm a university student, and I lost $3,000 on QuadrigaCX. That was my entire savings. I'm heartbroken and unsure of what to do next." - User on Reddit
- "I had 20 BTC on QuadrigaCX, and now it's gone. I feel so helpless and angry. This is a huge loss for me and a major setback for the crypto community." - User on Bitcointalk forum
- "I lost 2 BTC on QuadrigaCX. That was my entire investment in crypto. I don't think I can trust any exchange again after this experience." - User on Reddit

These tales of FTX, Mt. Gox, and QuadrigaCX underscore the importance of self-custody in protecting your crypto assets. With the US government currently taking action against leading exchanges like Coinbase and Binance, the case for self-custody becomes even more compelling. Don't gamble with your crypto; be your own bank, and ensure your financial future remains secure in the ever-evolving world of cryptocurrencies.

The Government Crackdown on Crypto

The exchange collapses mentioned above failed largely due to greed or technical factors involving their operations. However, there is an ever-larger negative force going after exchanges (and all aspects of crypto) – government. The government is aware of how fragile fiat is, and they are also aware that crypto poses an existential threat that will quicken their demise.

Cryptocurrencies like Bitcoin can provide a haven and place to safeguard your wealth when the value of the US dollar plummets, and hyperinflation ensues. Governments don't want you to have an alternative, because they want you on your knees when they swoop down with 'CBDC's to the rescue'. They are now scrambling to suppress and control the burgeoning crypto industry, fearing the collapse of their carefully curated financial systems. Don't fall for their deception.

In the not-so-distant past, we witnessed the government's attempt to suffocate the financial lifeline of certain industries through the infamous Operation Choke Point. Operation Chokepoint was a U.S. government initiative that began in 2013, aimed at fighting financial fraud and other illegal activities. The idea was to put pressure on banks and payment processors to stop doing business with certain types of companies that were considered "high risk" for fraud, such as payday lenders, gun sellers, and adult entertainment businesses.

The government wanted to "choke off" these businesses' access to financial services, making it difficult for them to operate. While the goal was to target illegal activities, in typical government form, the initiative unfairly impacted legitimate businesses as well, making it harder for them to access banking services. Operation Chokepoint was officially discontinued in 2017 due to the controversy surrounding its tactics and impact on legal businesses.

Brian Wise, Senior Advisor for the U.S. Consumer Coalition, an organization that opposed Operation Chokepoint stated: "By secretly enlisting the help of banks and payment processors, the Department of Justice has essentially forced industries it doesn't like out of business." Among the industries targeted were payday lenders, firearm dealers, and online gambling sites. In a dramatic case, Peggy Craig, owner of Michael's Pawn and Gun in Fruitland, Florida, describes her experience with Operation Chokepoint: "Operation Chokepoint has been a nightmare for me and my business. I've been forced to close my doors for days at a time because my credit card processor has shut me down. I've lost customers because they can't use their credit cards to buy guns from me. And I'm worried that I'm going to have to close my business altogether if this keeps up."

Fast forward to the present, as fiat currencies falter, the government has launched a new offensive: Choke Point 2.0, targeting the crypto industry. The following list highlights 10 types of government actions being taken to stop crypto, along with examples of individuals and companies experiencing each type of action:

- Regulatory crackdowns: Binance, accused of money laundering and criminal activity.
- Legal battles: LBRY, faced a multi-year high-profile lawsuit from the SEC (see the story later in this chapter)
- Tax enforcement: IRS ramping up efforts to tax cryptocurrency transactions and obtain individual transaction data from exchanges.
- Banking restrictions: Crypto exchanges facing difficulties in maintaining banking relationships.

- Travel bans: Industry leaders, such as Changpeng Zhao (CZ) of Binance, face travel restrictions.
- International sanctions: The government has started to use sanctions against the use of crypto currency (North Korea and Iran)
- Direct asset seizures: US authorities seize billions in cryptocurrency from "criminal" operations.
- National security concerns: TikTok, a popular social media platform, scrutinized for its potential ties to the Chinese government and cryptocurrency promotion leading to the proposed RESTRICT Act.
- Central Bank Digital Currencies (CBDCs): Governments developing their own digital currencies to maintain control.
- Internet censorship: China's Great Firewall blocking access to foreign cryptocurrency exchanges.

Since getting involved with crypto in New Hampshire, I have met many early adopters and pioneers in crypto. Within the past 12 months, two people that I know personally have experienced the full weight of the US government against them – for two completely unrelated (but pro-freedom) applications of cryptocurrency – LBRY and the Crypto 6.

The SEC vs. LBRY

Allow me to introduce you to LBRY, a groundbreaking platform that aims to offer a beacon of free speech in an increasingly censored digital landscape. Picture a world where YouTube, one of the internet's most ubiquitous video-sharing platforms, has a worthy rival that embraces decentralization and resists censorship. That's

LBRY in a nutshell. It's a platform I'm proud to count myself among over a million registered users.

The concept of LBRY came to life in the wake of the worrying trend of tech giants wielding their power to silence voices they deem unfit for their platforms. It's an alarming reality highlighted by none other than tech maestro Elon Musk, whose exposé, "The Twitterfiles," unveiled the dark underbelly of big tech censorship.

However, LBRY's journey hasn't been smooth sailing. The platform's native token, LBC, found itself in the crosshairs of the SEC, the US Securities and Exchange Commission. This regulatory body waged a grueling five-year legal battle against LBRY, arguing that LBC was a security. The whole ordeal mirrored the absurdity and endless bureaucracy in Franz Kafka's "The Trial."
The verdict? Unfortunately for LBRY and its enthusiastic user base, the SEC won the lengthy legal skirmish. The repercussions of this decision are far from insignificant. LBRY's CEO, Jeremy Kaufman, voiced his concerns post-trial, stating, "The SEC vs. LBRY case establishes a precedent that threatens the entire US cryptocurrency industry. Under this standard, almost every cryptocurrency, including Ethereum and Doge, are securities."

Kaufman's words ring alarm bells for the future of crypto. They suggest that the fate of cryptocurrencies now hangs in the balance, teetering precariously on the whims of a regulatory body arguably more formidable than the SEC: the US Congress. This debacle serves as a stark reminder of the threats facing the crypto industry and the importance of vigilance in protecting our digital freedoms.

At the heart of the compelling and disconcerting saga known as the Crypto 6, we find Ian Freeman, a tireless advocate for freedom and a prominent figure in New Hampshire's liberty movement. For over a decade, I've had the privilege to know Ian, who, along with his Free Talk Live co-host Mark Edge, first introduced me to the world of Bitcoin. Their influence extends far beyond the borders of New Hampshire as they've been the frontline warriors of the liberty movement.

The Crypto 6 case, a federal criminal prosecution in the United States, revolves around six individuals, including Ian, who were integral to the Free Keene movement in Keene, New Hampshire. As libertarian activists, they ardently believed in the transformational potential of cryptocurrencies like Bitcoin to establish a decentralized and more private financial system. In pursuit of this goal, they facilitated the conversion of U.S. dollars to Bitcoin and visa versa.

However, in March 2021, their lives took a sudden turn as the FBI conducted sweeping raids on their residences and places of work. The charges were severe: operating an unlicensed money transmitting business and money laundering via Bitcoin. The defendants refuted these allegations, maintaining they didn't run an unlicensed money transmission operation as they levied no fees for their services. They also denied money laundering charges, asserting they merely facilitated the exchange of Bitcoin for U.S. dollars.

Despite these defenses, the government was unrelenting. They held that the defendants' actions of exchanging Bitcoin for U.S. dollars on behalf of third parties amounted to running an unlicensed money transmitting operation. They further claimed that by using Bitcoin, the defendants obscured the proceeds of crime, constituting money laundering.

A grueling two-week trial resulted in a guilty verdict on all counts. The defendants were handed down prison sentences potentially ranging from 18 months to a staggering 70 years. The Crypto 6 case is a landmark event, marking one of the first instances in the United States where Bitcoin usage led to criminal prosecution. The stark reality of this case is that individuals are now serving jail time for merely facilitating the exchange of Bitcoin for fiat currency. This stands as a grim testament to the lengths the authorities are willing to go to maintain control over financial systems.

As we reach the end of this chapter, let us take a moment to reflect on the monumental shift that cryptocurrencies, particularly Bitcoin, represent in the global financial landscape. We live in a world where governments attempt to control and regulate this emerging asset class, as they recognize the potential challenge it poses to traditional fiat currencies and centralized control. It is crucial, however, to remember the famous quote: "First they ignore you, then they laugh at you, then they fight you, then you win." We now stand at the "fight" stage, and it is imperative that we arm ourselves with knowledge to navigate these turbulent waters.

Crypto pioneers like the people of El Salvador have shown us that despite the adversity and skepticism, there is hope and progress. As more countries begin to consider embracing cryptocurrencies and their potential, we see the resilience and adaptability of these decentralized assets in the face of skepticism and regulatory challenges.

The trials faced by individuals and companies such as Ian Freeman and LBRY should serve as a clarion call to the crypto community. Now is the time for us to stand united, resilient, and fearless in the pursuit of decentralized, censorship-resistant technology. With every challenge, the crypto industry grows stronger, more innovative, and more dedicated to creating a better financial future for all.

It is essential not to be disheartened by the government's attempts to suppress cryptocurrencies. Instead, let us view these efforts as proof that the battle for financial freedom and decentralization is more critical now than ever before. We, the crypto community, must remain committed to forging a better, more inclusive financial system for all.

The revolution is happening right now, and you can be a part of it! Appendix A provides a comprehensive guide to safely purchasing and self-custodianing the cryptocurrencies discussed in this chapter. Even those with minimal technical knowledge can confidently join the world of crypto in under 15 minutes. Don't let fear or uncertainty hold you back from taking control of your financial future in the face of failing fiat currencies and intrusive government intervention.

Together, we will create a brighter, more decentralized future where financial freedom is not just a dream but a reality for all.

Key Takeaways from Chapter 6:

- Not all cryptocurrencies are created equal. When contemplating replacements for fiat currency, it's worth considering cryptocurrencies backed by the Proof-of-Work mechanism over Proof-of-Stake. This is because they generally provide more security and decentralization. Additionally, cryptocurrencies that haven't participated in questionable ICOs and maintain a decentralized organizational structure should be prioritized. Some examples include Bitcoin, Bitcoin Cash, Bitcoin SV, Litecoin, and Ravencoin.

- Privacy-focused cryptocurrencies like Monero and Zcash merit serious thought, especially in an era of increasing government scrutiny and surveillance. These digital assets offer heightened transactional privacy, which could be essential for preserving individual freedoms in the face of growing censorship.
- The crypto industry faces numerous challenges, including notorious exchange scandals and government crackdowns.
- Self-custody is essential for protecting crypto assets in an uncertain regulatory environment.
- Governments attempt to suppress and control the crypto industry through various measures, such as Choke Point 2.0.
- Companies and individuals, like LBRY and the Crypto 6, face regulatory adversity while pushing the boundaries of decentralized technology.
- Central Bank Digital Currencies (CBDCs) aim to tighten government control over the financial system, posing a threat to financial freedom.
- Nations embracing cryptocurrency, like El Salvador, demonstrate resilience and adaptability in the face of adversity.
- It's crucial for individuals to join the crypto revolution and seize control of their financial future amidst faltering fiat currencies and encroaching government intervention.

Artwork:

"Gold is money. Everything else is credit." - J.P. Morgan

In the realm of gold, a story unfolds,
Of power and wealth, as history has told.
Debasements and fraud, in shadows they dwell,
But self-custody shines, a truth to quell.

Fort Knox mysteries and FDR's decree,
A call for the wise, to hold gold and be free.
With knowledge in hand, and heartstrings entwined,
Golden wisdom we seek, and surely we'll find.

Chapter 7 Golden Wisdom: Unearthing the Secrets of Gold Ownership

The astonishing rise of cryptocurrencies, particularly decentralized ones like Bitcoin, heralds a new age of innovation and a potential escape from the inevitable downfall of fiat currency. While the digital realm holds immense potential, it is essential to recognize the ancient and unwavering allure of gold. As the quintessential symbol of wealth, power, and prestige throughout history, gold's gleaming yellow hue and resistance to corrosion have cemented its place as a treasured asset across civilizations and epochs. In this chapter, we embark on a captivating journey, traversing the annals of time to uncover gold's pivotal role in shaping the concept of sound money, its enduring significance, and how to make well-informed decisions when investing in this everlasting emblem of fortune.

Why This Chapter Matters

Recognizing gold's historical role as a store of value enables us to harness its enduring attributes to preserve wealth. Gaining insights into identifying trustworthy and reputable gold providers empowers us to make purchases confidently. Grasping the importance of self-custody for gold mitigates risks such as theft, fraud, and government confiscation. Learning how to manage and secure our gold holdings optimizes the benefits of this asset as a portfolio diversifier. Possessing tangible wealth in the form of gold fosters a sense of gratitude, wisdom, and stability amidst financial volatility.

Gold and its Historical Significance

From the pyramids of Egypt to the myths of ancient Greece and beyond, gold has always been a central player in our cultural narrative. The golden artifacts tucked away with Egyptian pharaohs were not just opulent trinkets but promises of a prosperous afterlife. The "Golden Fleece" of Greek legend wasn't merely a sought-after treasure but a symbol of divine power and authority. And let's not forget the South American civilizations like the Incas, who revered gold for its spiritual and religious resonance.

Consider the tale of King Midas, who was granted his wish that everything he touched would turn to gold. The tragic turn of events, as his cherished daughter and sustenance turned to the cold, hard metal, serves as a timeless parable of mankind's gold fever. It tells us, "Gold can indeed acquire anything, but it's only through wisdom that we can grasp its true worth."

Gold's saga as a monetary medium spans thousands of years, with different civilizations across the world embracing this precious metal as a standard currency. Whether it was ancient societies, the Lydians, the Roman Empire, or today's central banks, gold has been an indispensable tool for trade, providing a safety net of stability. This was the status quo until 1971, when President Nixon had the U.S. exit the gold standard, a move that many argue was a misstep that reverberates in our global monetary system even today.

Let's rewind to the 7th century BCE, to the kingdom of Lydia, present-day Turkey, where the first gold coins were minted. King Croesus is credited with this innovation, producing coins with intricate designs and uniform weights, thereby establishing a trustworthy trade system. The historian Herodotus aptly sums it up, "In Lydia, gold was first minted for commerce, marking the birth of silver and gold coinage."

Fast forward to the Roman Empire, an economic powerhouse with an extensive reach, where gold coins were the order of the day. The aureus, a gold coin brought to life by Julius Caesar, eased trade across the empire, fostering wealth and equilibrium. As the Roman scholar Pliny the Elder once noted, "Gold is the king of all kings."

In more recent times, central banks have stepped up as the guardians of gold reserves. Take, for example, the Federal Reserve, established in 1913, which was entrusted with holding and managing the U.S.'s gold reserves.

The Abuse and Debasement of Gold

Gold's extensive history as a reliable form of money speaks volumes about its inherent worth and timeless allure. However, this journey has been punctuated by trials and tribulations. While gold itself has always been a trusted medium of exchange, the way we've managed it has often proved problematic.

Take, for example, the historical debasement of gold coins, which often precipitated political and economic calamities. This was seen in the Roman Empire, where emperors diminished the gold content of coins to finance wars, and in the Byzantine Empire, where a similar debasement occurred. The Spanish Empire also faced a challenge when a flood of gold from the New World led to uncontrolled inflation. England's King Henry VIII was notorious for significantly reducing the gold and silver content in coins to sustain extravagant spending and military campaigns, leading to the manifestation of Gresham's Law, which states that "bad money drives out good."

Interestingly, the gold standard has dropped twice in recent times in favor of fiat currency. Modern economists, including Ben Bernanke, argue that breaking away from the gold standard helped speed up recovery from the Great Depression. However, advocates of the Austrian School of Economics, such as Murray Rothbard, maintain that leaving the gold standard resulted in even more severe economic upheavals. Germany's early departure from the gold standard is often pointed out as a factor that contributed to the rise of the Third Reich and the initiation of World War II. As British historian Niall Ferguson observed, "The disintegration of the international monetary system in the early 1930s, characterized by competitive devaluations and currency blocs, played a significant role in the slide into World War II."

A comparable scenario has been playing out since Nixon abandoned the gold standard in 1971, primarily to fund the Vietnam War, stimulate the economy, and tackle inflation. The aftermath has been marked by telltale signs of a failing fiat currency: increased economic instability, a weakening of international cooperation, the emergence of protectionist policies, heightened militarism, and a resurgence of nationalism.

Today, we teeter on the brink of a third World War with adversaries like Russia and China, while countries such as Russia, China, India, and Brazil are distancing themselves from the dollar at an alarming rate. Financial analyst and economist Martin Armstrong warns, "We are teetering on the edge of World War III. The conflict in Ukraine is merely the tip of the iceberg. The war will likely expand to other regions. Gold is the safest investment for those seeking to safeguard their wealth during these unstable times. Gold is a physical asset that can't be easily devalued or inflated away."

Buying Power

It's become almost second nature for us to accept an annual inflation rate of 2-3% as the norm. Yet, the subtle reality of this slow-burning inflation is that the dollar in your pocket is continually losing its worth as time goes by. The tables below illustrate a striking truth: fiat currencies persistently depreciate in value, while gold has consistently demonstrated its ability to retain purchasing power across history. This underscores gold's attractiveness as a potentially more stable means of safeguarding wealth.

Item	1913 Price	Recent Price
Car	$600	$37,000
Home	$3,500	$287,000
Education (Annual College Tuition)	$75	$26,000
Gallon of Milk	$0.36	$3.50
Loaf of Bread	$0.06	$2.50
Movie Ticket	$0.10	$9.50
Suit	$15	$650

The dwindling purchasing power of the US dollar isn't an isolated phenomenon; other fiat currencies have also witnessed comparable erosions in value (think of images of Berliners carting wheelbarrows of cash or that staggering $100 trillion Zimbabwean bill)!

Meanwhile, gold has largely managed to maintain its purchasing power over centuries, if not millennia. The table below effectively underscores the comparative stability of gold's purchasing power across a variety of goods and time periods:

Goods	Ancient Time Range	Ancient Price (oz of gold)	Modern Price (oz of gold)
High-quality Toga	Ancient Rome (753 BC - 476 AD)	0.6	1
Loaf of Bread	Ancient Egypt (3000 BC - 30 BC)	0.02	0.01
High-quality Wine	Ancient Greece (8th-6th century BC)	0.5	0.3
Bolt of Silk	Ancient China (2700 BC - 221 BC)	5	4
Pound of Spices	Medieval Europe (5th-15th century AD)	0.5	0.3

Indeed, like any market, the gold sector has not been immune to its share of problems. Predominantly, the challenges encountered have been tied to third parties, governmental actions, and marketplace misconduct. Given that gold is a tangible asset, somewhat cumbersome to move around, and its supply isn't unlimited, the market remains vulnerable to manipulation and other undesirable activities. Let's delve into four instances of manipulation and scandals that have tarnished the image of gold over time.

Gold Market Manipulation

Market manipulation encompasses a variety of tactics intended to artificially impact gold prices. Some of the most common strategies include:

- Spoofing: This involves placing substantial orders without the genuine intention of carrying them out, thus creating a deceptive image of demand or supply.
- Wash trading: This strategy involves the simultaneous buying and selling of the same asset, creating an illusion of extensive trading volume.
- Cornering: This involves amassing a significant share of the market supply with the aim of controlling and manipulating the price.

The collapse of the London Gold Pool in 1968 underscores the issues with gold market manipulation and the involvement of central banks.

In the early 1960s, the United States and several European countries set up the London Gold Pool to uphold the fixed gold price of $35 per ounce, as stipulated by the Bretton Woods system. The participating central banks agreed to consolidate their gold reserves and transact gold in the market to maintain price stability. However, as the U.S. dollar grappled with escalating inflation due to mounting government expenditure, especially towards the Vietnam War and social programs, a growing disparity emerged between the official gold price and its actual market value.

In March 1968, the London Gold Pool encountered a crisis as gold demand soared, fueled by concerns about the stability of the U.S. dollar. Speculators began to buy gold in large quantities, wagering that the central banks could not sustain the $35 per ounce price, and indeed, it spiked to $43.50 per ounce – a significant premium. As gold reserves depleted, the member countries of the London Gold Pool decided to cease their market intervention efforts, culminating in the collapse of the London Gold Pool on March 17, 1968.

The aftermath of the London Gold Pool's collapse led to a bifurcated gold market system, with an official price for central bank transactions and a free-floating market price for private transactions. This development marked the beginning of the end for the Bretton Woods system, which eventually gave way to a system of floating exchange rates in 1971.

Reflecting upon the collapse of the London Gold Pool, former Governor of the Bank of England, Lord George, observed, "The London Gold Pool could not withstand the onslaught of market forces, which proved to be far more potent than the central banks."

Fraudulent Activities in the Gold Market:

Fraudulent operations in the gold market can take on many forms, such as Ponzi schemes, counterfeit gold, and deceptive mining operations. The scandal involving Bre-X Minerals in the mid-1990s stands as a stark example of such fraudulent activities in the gold market.

Bre-X, a Canadian mining company, announced a seemingly monumental discovery - the world's largest gold deposit in Busang, Indonesia. However, the entire operation eventually unraveled as a complex fraud. Under the leadership of CEO David Walsh, geologist John Felderhof, and project manager Michael de Guzman, Bre-X Minerals reported the discovery of a vast gold deposit nestled in the Indonesian jungles. Consequently, the company's stock price experienced a meteoric rise, with the company's market capitalization exceeding $6 billion. This mirage of immense wealth attracted investors, banks, and even the Indonesian government.

Nonetheless, the supposed gold deposit was nothing more than an elaborate hoax, concocted by the company's employees who had been "salting" the core samples with gold procured from local sources. When the truth surfaced in 1997, the company's stock price plummeted, resulting in significant financial losses for thousands of investors. This scandal sent shockwaves through the mining industry, leading to more rigorous scrutiny and tightened regulations for mining companies.

Moreover, the Bre-X debacle significantly damaged the reputation of the Canadian mining industry and the Toronto Stock Exchange, where the company's shares were listed. The magnitude of the Bre-X scandal is encapsulated in a statement by Nick Barisheff, CEO of Bullion Management Group, who remarked, "Bre-X serves as the ultimate example of 'buyer beware.' Here you had the biggest fraud in mining history, all predicated on something that simply didn't exist."

Physical Manipulation of the Gold Market

Manipulation of the physical gold market can entail activities such as gold smuggling, refining to eliminate impurities, and illegal mining. One of the most intriguing and sinister stories in this regard is that of Nazi Gold.

During their conquest of much of Europe, the Nazis seized enormous quantities of gold, currency, artwork, and other precious items. These were taken from central banks, private individuals, and particularly Jewish families targeted during the Holocaust. The stolen assets were instrumental in financing the Nazi war machine and bolstering its economic prowess.

A considerable fraction of the appropriated gold was reprocessed by the Nazi regime. They melted it down and stored it in the Reichsbank's vaults in Berlin, as well as other locations throughout Germany and its occupied territories. A significant amount of this stolen gold was subsequently transferred to Swiss banks, where it was traded for hard currency to sustain the Nazi war effort.

At the culmination of World War II, Allied forces unearthed and reclaimed a substantial portion of the pilfered gold. The Tripartite Commission for the Restitution of Monetary Gold, established by the United States, the United Kingdom, and France, was charged with the task of returning the recovered gold to its rightful owners or their respective governments. Nevertheless, the precise quantity of stolen gold and the location of all assets remain uncertain to this day.

The tale of Nazi Gold is not merely a narrative of avarice and grand-scale theft, but also a grim reminder of the human suffering inflicted by the Holocaust. In the years following the war, considerable efforts have been made to locate and recover the stolen gold and other assets to provide restitution to Holocaust survivors and their families.

The story has further sparked discussions about the role of Swiss banks and other financial institutions that may have consciously or inadvertently aided the Nazi regime's operations. In his book "Nazi Gold: The Full Story of the Fifty-Year Swiss-Nazi Conspiracy to Steal Billions from Europe's Jews and Holocaust Survivors," Tom Bower underscores the magnitude of the theft: "The scale of the looting was unprecedented, amounting to billions of dollars' worth of gold, banknotes, and other valuables. Central to the looting process was the confiscation of gold, which was melted down and recast into ingots bearing the official German stamp."

Central Bank Manipulation of the Gold Market

Central bank intervention in the gold market can entail activities such as gold sales, gold leasing, and the determination of official gold prices. A prime illustration of the profound influence central bank policy can have on gold markets is the "Brown Bottom" incident in 1999. During this event, the UK Chancellor of the Exchequer, Gordon Brown, declared intentions to sell off a significant part of the country's gold reserves.

In May 1999, Brown announced the UK's plan to sell approximately 58% of its gold reserves (roughly 415 tons) over a few years to diversify the nation's foreign exchange holdings. This decision sparked controversy, particularly as it was taken when gold prices were close to their 20-year low. The auctions commenced in July 1999 and extended until 2002, with the gold being sold at an average price of around $275 per ounce.

The declaration and subsequent sales were dubbed the "Brown Bottom" as they contributed to driving gold prices to record lows. Many criticized the decision, arguing that the sales were ill-timed and ultimately led to the UK losing out on billions of dollars in potential revenue. In the years that followed the gold sales, gold prices saw a substantial rebound, reaching new record highs of $2080 per ounce in May 2023. The "Brown Bottom" incident also caused other central banks to reevaluate their gold reserve management strategies, leading many to reduce or stop their gold sales.

Reflecting on the "Brown Bottom" gold sales, Peter Hambro, the founder of the UK-based gold mining company Petropavlovsk, remarked, "It was an utterly misguided move. The decision was made by a man who lacked an understanding of the gold market, and it was a genuine tragedy for the country."

The Importance of Self-custody

The multitude of risk factors and uncertainties characterizing the gold market underscore the significance of maintaining self-custody of gold, as opposed to placing trust in third parties. Let's explore the different risk factors associated with non-custodial gold.

The five principal categories of risk factors in relation to non-custodial gold encompass theft or loss, counterfeit gold, physical damage or degradation, disputes over ownership, and government seizure or confiscation.

Non-custodial Risk Factors	Tangible Examples
Theft or loss	1. Brink's-Mat Robbery: Thieves stole £26 million worth of gold bullion in 1983.
	2. Central Bank of Iraq Heist: Approximately $1 billion in cash, gold, and other valuables were stolen in 2003.
	3. Hatton Garden Heist: Thieves stole gold, diamonds, and other valuables worth up to £200 million in 2015.
Counterfeit gold	1. Fake Perth Mint Gold Bars: Counterfeit gold bars bearing the Perth Mint logo were discovered in 2018.
	2. Gold-plated Tungsten Scam: Tungsten bars coated in gold were passed off as genuine gold bars.
	3. Fake PAMP Suisse Gold Bars: High-quality counterfeit gold bars mimicking the PAMP Suisse brand surfaced in the market.
Physical damage or degradation	1. Gold Smuggling in Rectum: Gold smugglers were caught in Sri Lanka with gold bars hidden in their rectums, leading to damaged and contaminated gold.
	2. Gold Bar Corrosion: Gold bars stored in humid conditions developed rust-like spots, reducing their value.
	3. Gold Bar Discoloration: A gold bar stored in a PVC container developed green discoloration due to chemical reactions.
Ownership dispute	1. SS Central America Shipwreck: Ownership disputes arose over $150 million worth of recovered gold from the 1857 shipwreck.
	2. Nazi Gold Train: A rumored train filled with Nazi gold has led to multiple ownership claims and disputes.
	3. Gold Inheritance Battle: A family fought in court over a $1.2 million gold inheritance left by their deceased relative.
Government seizure or confiscation	1. FDR's Gold Confiscation: President Roosevelt ordered Americans to surrender their gold in 1933.
	2. Venezuelan Gold Seizure: The Bank of England refused to return $1.2 billion in gold to Venezuela in 2018.
	3. Turkish Gold Seizure: The Turkish government seized gold owned by individuals accused of financing terrorism in 2017.

When we talk about self-custody, we truly mean self-custody. We live in a time where trust in large institutions is experiencing a significant decline. Bank safe deposit boxes, exchange-traded funds, or even gold purportedly held by central banks cannot be taken at face value. Self-custody implies direct control and possession.

All the gold in Fort Knox?

Do central banks truly possess the gold they claim to have? Let's delve into the story of Fort Knox and its gold. In the 1970s, several congress members made a trip to Fort Knox to authenticate the gold reserves. However, they were reportedly not shown any gold, sparking conspiracy theories about what the vault really contains. One flabbergasted congressman purportedly exclaimed, "We came all this way and they won't even show us the gold!"

In the 1960s and '70s, when France demanded gold in return for US dollars, the then French President Charles de Gaulle famously declared, "We want the gold, not the paper." John Connally, US Treasury Secretary at the time, retorted, "The dollar is our currency, but your problem." This event ultimately led President Nixon to abandon the gold standard in 1971.

To this day, the amount of gold in Fort Knox remains a closely guarded secret. Estimates vary between 140 million and 200 million ounces. The US Government Accountability Office (GAO) conducts audits of Fort Knox. However, it's worth noting that this is the same government that has misplaced trillions of dollars in defense spending. Interestingly, despite the GAO's recommendations in 2012 and 2019 regarding inventory management and procedures for tracking gold and silver bullion movement, Fort Knox hasn't fully implemented them all. As former congressman Ron Paul stated, "There is a lack of transparency at the Fed and with our gold holdings. The American people have a right to know. We should have a full accounting, and we should be able to depend on the truth of what our government is telling us."

In our current era, the larger the organization, the less trustworthy it tends to be.

Franklin D. Roosevelt (FDR) Gold Confiscation

If you think the government won't come after your gold, think again. The shocking story of FDR's gold confiscation stresses the importance of self-custody and highlights the risks of using third party custodians. In 1933, President Franklin D. Roosevelt issued Executive Order 6102, requiring Americans to surrender their gold holdings to the government. The magnitude of this confiscation was immense, with citizens being forced to exchange their gold for paper currency at a fixed rate. One man, who had inherited a substantial gold collection from his grandfather, recalled the event: "I couldn't believe it was happening in America. We had to hand over our family's gold legacy just like that." The government didn't go door to door confiscating gold. They largely seized gold from banks and third-party custodians and relied on individual citizens to voluntarily relinquish their gold at $35/ounce. In short, in time of stress and government confiscation, you want to retain the power to say "No" and hold on to your gold.

Considering the various risks associated with non-custodial gold and the broader market manipulations and fraud, self-custody is critical. By maintaining possession of your gold, you can mitigate the risks of theft, counterfeiting, damage, ownership disputes, and government confiscation. So, remember to keep your gold close, and your trust in third parties closer!

In this chapter, we have delved into the intriguing world of gold, examining its historical importance and various challenges that have emerged throughout time. We have explored the gold market's manipulation, fraud, and other issues, while emphasizing the significance of self-custody.

In Chapter 11, I provide a list of criteria to be used when buying self-custody gold, along with a guide of national vendors for purchasing self-custody gold, ensuring that you can find a reliable and trustworthy source for your precious metal investments.

Key Takeaways from Chapter 7:

- Gold's longevity as a form of currency and store of value is a testament to its dependability. Its steadfast performance throughout history is truly unmatched.
- The gold market hasn't been immune to issues like market manipulation and fraud, highlighting the importance of self-custody as a risk mitigation strategy. Regulatory supervision has proven to be inadequate in this regard.
- Possessing gold without actual custody carries a variety of risks, ranging from theft and counterfeiting to ownership disputes and even governmental confiscation. Opting for direct ownership is a strategy that can help curtail these potential hazards.
- Self-custody empowers investors with absolute control over their gold, reducing third-party-

related risks and fostering personal responsibility and accountability.

- Past events, such as the Fort Knox saga and FDR's gold confiscation, serve as stark reminders of the risks associated with entrusting third parties with gold storage. They underscore the necessity of self-custody in an environment where governments may seize opportunities at the expense of the individual.
- For those interested in purchasing self-custody gold, Chapter 11 provides a detailed criterion and a list of trustworthy vendors, aiding in making informed and secure purchase decisions.
- Learning and implementing the right techniques for managing and securing self-custody gold assets enhances benefits while decreasing risks. Adhering to best practices fortifies protection.

Artwork:

"The best thing one can do when it's raining is to let it rain and look for the silver lining." - Henry Wadsworth Longfellow

In the gleam of silver's light,
A tale unfolds of wealth and might.
From ancient coins to modern tech,
Its allure and power we must not forget.

A rival to gold, the stories unfold,
Of battles and victories, both new and old.
Through scandals and swindles, we learn and grow,
The importance of self-custody, a truth we must know.

With wisdom in hand, we stride with grace,
In a world where silver finds its place.
Our hearts enlightened, grateful, and bold,
We embrace the journey, as the story's told.

Chapter 8: Silver: A Journey Through Time, Value, and Scandals

Now that we've shed light on self-custody crypto and gold as reliable alternatives to the unstable world of fiat currencies, it's time to introduce another option into our roster. Say hello to the dazzling universe of silver! This precious metal, which has captured human imagination for thousands of years, has played an integral part in our shared past. Its reflective, conductive, and antibacterial attributes have rendered it indispensable across a vast range of sectors, spanning electronics and solar energy to healthcare. Not to mention silver's notable role as a wealth preserver and a safeguard against economic instability.

While gold has traditionally been the showstopper in the precious metals arena, silver has been its more pragmatic, yet equally enchanting sibling. Even though silver usually holds a lesser value than gold, it possesses its own distinct benefits, such as being more cost-effective and adaptable for industrial uses. To assist you in traversing the gleaming landscape of silver, we'll delve into its various aspects throughout this chapter, guiding you through its history, market intricacies, and the significance of self-custody.

Why This Chapter Matters

Acknowledging silver's longstanding role as a store of value equips us to leverage its proven attributes for wealth preservation. Understanding how to distinguish reliable and reputable silver providers allows us to undertake purchases with assurance. Comprehending the significance of self-custody for silver shields against risks like theft, fraud, and government seizure. Acquiring the skills to manage and secure our silver assets maximizes their advantages as portfolio diversifiers. Having tangible wealth in the form of silver nurtures a sense of gratitude, wisdom, and groundedness in the face of financial turbulence.

Silver: A Shining Thread Through History

From ancient Egypt to modern Europe, silver has captivated and dazzled cultures throughout history. This lustrous metal has woven a story of religion, art, and power, leaving an indelible mark on human civilization.

In ancient Egypt, Greece, and Rome, silver transcended mere currency, becoming an integral part of art and sacred rituals. Egyptians revered silver as a sacred metal linked to the moon, crafting exquisite adornments for their pharaohs. The Greeks, valuing its beauty, incorporated silver into pottery and sculptures. Roman Emperor Nero, infamous for his extravagant spending, took his obsession with silver to new heights – constructing a palace made entirely of the metal and showering his guests with silver and gold petals.

Silver's divine connection spans religious traditions, including Christianity and Hinduism, where it is used to create sacred objects and vessels. The myth of the silver thread, an unbreakable connection between mortals and the divine, has been shared across cultures, symbolizing the eternal bond.

In China, silver served as both currency and a symbol of wealth, with Ming Dynasty artisans creating intricate sculptures and jewelry for nobility. The legend of the Silver Pagoda tells the tale of a pious merchant who, after a dream of Buddha, built a temple with a pure silver roof, turning it into a pilgrimage site for Buddhists from all over China.

Europe's silver story is one of art, fashion, and luxury, as the Renaissance saw silver incorporated into breathtaking works of art and opulent, silver-threaded fabrics. The Spanish conquest of the Americas reveals the European obsession with silver, which led them to the mines of Potosi in modern-day Bolivia – a treasure trove that fueled their empire.

From sacred rituals to grand palaces, silver's glimmer has captured our imaginations throughout history, tying us together through a shining thread that weaves an enchanting tale of beauty, wealth, and divine connection.

Silver Currency: The Glittering Legacy of Empires

Silver has historically acted as a cornerstone of currency, influencing trade and economic dynamics across a multitude of civilizations. From the era of Ancient Rome to the reign of the Spanish Empire, this precious metal has left an enduring impact on global trade.

Ancient Rome was instrumental in revolutionizing currency with its standardized silver coins. These coins, minted in large quantities and endorsed for purity by the state, facilitated transactions across the Mediterranean world, including purchasing goods and remitting taxes. In fact, the saying "paying through the nose" originated from Roman tax collectors gripping a taxpayer's nose to guarantee complete payment.

The Spanish Empire, empowered by the abundant silver mines in the Americas, established the Spanish silver dollar, or the "piece of eight," as a globally recognized currency, drastically transforming global trade. Spanish silver coins remained a foundational element of international trade until the 19th century. The quest for this gleaming treasure is encapsulated in English privateer Sir Francis Drake's words, "Santiago and a hundred other saints guide us! Will this voyage make us all rich men, or will it send us to the bottom of the sea with our pockets full of Spanish silver?"

The Bimetallic standard, which involved the use of both gold and silver as legal tender at fixed relative values, further exemplifies silver's role in currency. Widely implemented in the 19th century, this system allowed countries to maintain stable currencies and promote international trade.

The allure of silver has steered the rise and fall of empires, from Ancient Rome to the Spanish Empire. Its radiant legacy, intertwined with its cultural significance and practical applications, solidifies silver's position as a timeless and invaluable asset throughout history. The following table provides a summarized depiction of the utilization of silver as currency across historical eras.

Historical Era	Silver as Currency
Ancient Egypt	Silver was used as currency for trade and payment of taxes
Ancient Greece	Silver was used as currency, and silver coins were minted in various city-states
Ancient Rome	Silver was used as currency and was the standard material for Roman currency
China	Silver was used as currency during various dynasties, including the Ming Dynasty
Spanish Empire	Silver was the main currency used for global trade during the colonial era
Bimetallic	A monetary standard in which the value of the monetary unit was based on gold and silver prices, used in various countries throughout history (including the United States)

The Battle of the Metals

As we've noted, silver and gold have a storied history serving as money and stores of value for countless generations. Nonetheless, there has always existed a spirited debate between proponents of the two precious metals, often leading to fervent confrontations. In this segment, we'll delve into the historical friction and alliances between advocates of silver and gold.

Uses as Money

When contemplating the use of silver and gold as forms of money, it's important to acknowledge both their parallels and contrasts. Both metals have served as mediums of exchange for millennia, thanks to their lasting nature, scarcity, and ability to be divided. Yet, gold boasts a higher value per weight unit compared to silver, making it more fitting for sizeable exchanges. Conversely, silver's greater abundance relative to gold renders it more attainable for smaller transactions.

Properties, Roles in the Global Economy, and Uses as Store of Value

Now, let's delve deeper into the characteristics, economic roles, and functions as value preservers for silver and gold. The following table encapsulates the primary similarities and disparities between these two precious metals.

Dimension	Silver	Gold
Rarity	More abundant	Rarer
Value	Lower	Higher
Monetary Unit	Smaller denominations, suited for everyday use	Larger denominations, suited for large trades
Historical Use	Widely used in ancient and modern currencies	Widely used in ancient and modern currencies
Coinage History	Roman denarius, Spanish pieces of eight	Ancient Greek staters, British gold sovereigns
Symbolism	Associated with the moon, femininity	Associated with the sun, masculinity
Market Price Stability	Less stable due to industrial demand	More stable
Industrial & Technological Applications	Extensive applications in electronics, photography, and medicine	Limited applications in electronics, aerospace, and medicine
Storage & Transport	Less dense, larger volumes needed for storage	Denser, more compact storage
Central Bank Reserves	Smaller proportion of global reserves	Larger proportion of global reserves
Bimetallism	Part of the Bimetallic standard	Part of the Bimetallic standard

Battles between Silver and Gold Supporters

As evident from the above table, silver and gold share numerous commonalities yet also display distinct differences. Historical records reveal numerous clashes between the advocates of silver and gold, illustrating five such instances:

- The Coinage Act of 1834: This law altered the silver-to-gold ratio in the US, triggering discontent among silver proponents who feared the impact on their industry.

- The Free Silver Movement of the late 19th century: This political initiative pressed for unlimited silver coinage to expand the money supply, benefiting farmers and debtors.
- The Silver Purchase Act of 1934: This law sanctioned the US government's silver purchases, cheering silver industry stakeholders but irking gold advocates who viewed it as an inflation-boosting measure.
- The International Monetary Fund's decision to establish gold as the benchmark for its Special Drawing Rights in 1969: Silver enthusiasts disapproved of this decision, arguing that silver should have been included.
- The ongoing debate over reverting to the gold standard in the 2010s: This argument revolves around whether the US should reinstate the gold standard.

Perhaps the most heated confrontation between gold and silver supporters was the Free Silver Movement of the late 19th century, taking center stage in the 1896 election.

This crusade was spearheaded by William Jennings Bryan. In the US, the face-off between silver and gold proponents reached a fever pitch in the late 19th century. The Coinage Act of 1873, effectively demonetizing silver and instituting a gold standard, was seen as a triumph for gold advocates, who touted gold's stability and reliability as a store of value. However, silver backers vehemently objected, arguing the move would constrict the money supply, thus harming farmers and other debtors.

The conflict reached its zenith during the infamous 1896 presidential campaign between silver enthusiast William Jennings Bryan and gold supporter William McKinley. Bryan's memorable "Cross of Gold" speech at the Democratic National Convention still resonates, where he proclaimed, "We will answer their demand for a gold standard by saying to them: You shall not press down upon the brow of labor this crown of thorns; you shall not crucify mankind upon a cross of gold." Despite Bryan's fervent silver advocacy, he eventually conceded the election to McKinley, who maintained the gold standard.

Silver: The Powerhouse of Industrial Applications

Silver, the champion in electrical and thermal conductivity among metals, holds a coveted position thanks to its wide array of industrial uses. Its unparalleled properties have made it an irreplaceable resource in the electronics industry, where it is integral to key components in circuit boards, solar panels, and batteries. Similarly, the automobile industry heavily depends on silver for crucial elements like airbag sensors and switches.

Stepping away from electronics, silver's antimicrobial traits have ensured its continued use in the healthcare sector for centuries. Presently, silver nanoparticles find use in state-of-the-art medical practices, ranging from imaging to drug delivery. Thanks to its high reflectivity, silver is the go-to metal for mirrors, telescopes, and energy-efficient coatings on glass.

The charm of silver isn't limited to industrial applications; its pliability and shine make it a favored material for decorative purposes such as jewelry and silverware. However, what truly distinguishes silver from gold is the delicate balance between industrial demand and silver prices. In prosperous economic times, when industrial demand escalates, silver prices tend to rise, making it an appealing hedge against inflation. As financier Jim Rogers succinctly put it, "Inflation is the great destroyer of currencies. Silver, on the other hand, has been a store of value for centuries."

However, this relationship isn't simple, as shifts in industrial demand can directly sway silver prices. A decrease in demand could result in an oversupply, leading to price drops. Given its dynamic role across a multitude of industries — from electronics to healthcare — silver emerges as a versatile force, influencing the trajectory of technological advancement and economic stability.

Unveiling Silver Market Scandals: A Guide to Schemes and Swindles

The silver market, while enticing, has witnessed a range of scandals over the years. Understanding the types of market manipulation is key to protecting oneself and appreciating the colorful history of silver trading while stressing the importance of holding silver in your own custody (just as with cryptocurrency and gold).

Market manipulation is indeed a deceptive strategy where certain individuals or organizations indulge in activities that unnaturally depress or inflate the price of an asset, such as silver, for their own financial advantage. Let's delve into some of the most common market manipulation tactics:

1. **Spoofing:** This is a deceptive strategy that involves placing orders with no intention of executing them. The aim is to mislead other

194

market participants about the supply and demand of a particular asset, prompting them to trade based on false information, which in turn manipulates the asset's price in the spoofer's favor.

2. **Front-Running:** Front-running involves a broker or other market participant executing orders on a security for its own account while taking advantage of advanced knowledge of pending orders from its customers. In essence, they're "jumping the queue" to profit from the price move that will occur once the large pending orders are executed.

3. **Wash Trading:** This manipulation tactic involves an investor simultaneously selling and buying the same financial instruments to create misleading, artificial activity in the marketplace. This could give a false impression of voluminous activity for the asset, attracting other investors.

4. **Painting the Tape:** This strategy involves creating an illusion of activity by trading a particular asset among a group of colluding traders. The aim is to attract attention to the asset, encouraging other investors to buy in and drive up the price, at which point the colluding traders sell for a profit.

The Hunt Brothers' Silver Fiasco in 1980 serves as a prime example of market manipulation and its consequences.

The infamous Hunt brothers, Texas oil magnates Nelson Bunker Hunt, William Herbert Hunt, and Lamar Hunt, embarked on a mission to monopolize the silver market by hoarding an astonishing 75% of the global supply. Their journey began in the late 1970s when they began purchasing silver as a hedge against inflation. Their relentless acquisition of the precious metal propelled silver prices from a modest $6 per ounce in 1979 to an incredible peak of nearly $50 per ounce in January 1980.

This spectacle didn't go unnoticed by the US government and financial regulators. They grew increasingly alarmed by the potential fallout of such market manipulation. As a countermeasure, the Commodity Futures Trading Commission (CFTC) and other regulatory bodies implemented various restrictions, including hiking margin requirements for silver futures contracts, thereby making it costlier to maintain extensive market positions.

Amid the escalating silver crisis, Bunker Hunt defended their audacious actions in an interview, stating, "A billion dollars isn't what it used to be. If you're worth $3 billion, and you're not a Saudi sheik or a Chicago futures trader, you don't have the right to lose it." This statement underscores the brothers' resolute determination and their seeming indifference to the potential repercussions of their maneuvers.

The regulatory intervention sparked a rapid sell-off, triggering a catastrophic plunge in silver prices. The Hunt brothers eventually filed for bankruptcy. The notorious Silver Thursday market crash on March 27, 1980, serves as a stark reminder of the perils of market manipulation and the critical role of regulatory oversight in preserving the integrity and stability of financial markets.

Now, let's discuss Commodity Fraud, a type of financial crime that misleads investors by misrepresenting a commodity's quality or nature, such as silver. This umbrella term covers various deceitful schemes, including Ponzi schemes, affinity fraud, and high-pressure sales tactics. The Bullion Direct Commodity Fraud of 2016 provides a compelling case study.

Texas-based precious metals dealer Bullion Direct unexpectedly closed in 2015, leaving customers with millions of dollars in unfulfilled orders for gold, silver, and other precious metals. The company had been operating an online platform that facilitated the purchase, storage, and sale of physical precious metals. However, it was later revealed that Bullion Direct had been failing to meet customer orders, and the inventory supposedly stored on behalf of clients was largely non-existent.

The company's founder, Charles McAllister, was apprehended and charged with fraud in 2016 for diverting customer funds for personal expenditures and unrelated business ventures. After the scandal, one of the affected customers, Joe Blanton, lamented, "We trusted Bullion Direct because they had been around for a while, and everything seemed legitimate. But in the end, our trust was betrayed."

The Bullion Direct Commodity Fraud underscores the importance of conducting thorough due diligence when investing in commodities. It also highlights the need for robust regulatory oversight to identify and prevent fraudulent practices. Furthermore, it emphasizes the criticality of investor vigilance and the importance of collaborating with reputable and transparent companies to mitigate the risk of such schemes. This case indeed makes a compelling argument for self-custody!

Let's move on to Market Rigging, a deceptive strategy where individuals or organizations create false supply or demand indicators to manipulate prices for their benefit. Market rigging often involves tactics such as spoofing,

wash trading, and quote stuffing. One of the most remarkable instances of market rigging transpired in 2010 when JPMorgan Chase faced accusations of manipulating the silver market. Whistleblower Andrew Maguire, a former trader at Goldman Sachs, disclosed JPMorgan Chase's extensive role in rigging the silver market using deceptive practices like placing substantial orders and
then aborting them before execution, thus falsely inflating the perception of demand.

In a conversation with King World News, Maguire revealed, "JPMorgan acts as an agent for the Federal Reserve; they act to halt the rise of gold and silver against the US dollar. JPMorgan is insulated from potential losses [on their short positions] by the Fed and/or the U.S. taxpayer." This statement draws attention to the grave implications of the situation, suggesting not only that JPMorgan Chase's actions were manipulative but also potentially backed by powerful institutions.

Market manipulation, commodity fraud, and market rigging are deceptive practices that can have severe repercussions on investors and the overall stability of the financial markets stressing the need for self-custody.

The Importance of Self-custody

The annals of history are laden with instances where governments, in dire straits, resort to extreme measures. While the United States Government has historically only seized gold, it's essential to remain cognizant of the fact that escalating desperation could potentially lead to radical actions. This realization underscores the utmost importance of self-custody when it comes to your silver, akin to your gold and cryptocurrency. Trusting banks or even third-party storage facilities and dealers with the safekeeping of your silver can prove to be a risky venture. Here are three cautionary tales that drive this point home:

- Northwest Territorial Mint Bankruptcy (2016): Known for being a long-standing precious metals dealer and mint, Northwest Territorial Mint's bankruptcy in 2016 left customers in a lurch. Many who had purchased silver from the company and trusted them with its storage found themselves unable to retrieve their assets, resulting in the loss of their entire precious metals collections.
- Tulving Company Bankruptcy (2014): The Tulving Company, a distinguished dealer in gold, silver, and other precious metals, declared bankruptcy in 2014, leaving customers who had entrusted them with the storage of their metals facing substantial losses. Hannes Tulving Jr., the company's proprietor, faced charges of wire fraud and was subsequently sentenced to jail for swindling customers out of more than $15 million.
- GoldSilver.com Storage Scandal (2017): GoldSilver.com, an online precious metals dealer, came under fire in 2017 when customers discovered that the company had failed in its duty to properly store their silver and other metals. Customers who had paid for storage services found their holdings inadequately protected or insured, leading to significant financial losses.

In Chapter 11, we offer a comprehensive list of criteria for acquiring self-custody silver, alongside a ratings guide for top national vendors from whom you can purchase self-custody silver.

Key Takeaways from Chapter 8

- Silver has a rich history dating back thousands of years and has been used as a store of value and medium of exchange in many civilizations.
- The silver market is subject to various types of manipulation, including market rigging, market manipulation and commodity fraud.
- Despite the risks, self-custody silver can provide greater control and privacy over your silver holdings. When buying self-custody silver, look for reputable dealers, consider the form of silver (e.g. coins, bars, rounds), and make sure you have a secure storage location.
- Silver prices are affected by many factors, including supply and demand, industrial usage, economic conditions, and investor sentiment.
- With a basic understanding of the silver market and a thoughtful approach to investing, anyone can participate in this important asset class and potentially benefit from the advantages it offers.

Artwork:

"Fiat money is a currency without intrinsic value that has been established as money, often by government regulation." - Ludwig von Mises

In a world where money's changing fast,
The days of fiat, they may not last.
With CBDCs looming near,
Awareness and action must appear.

Gold and silver stand the test of time,
Crypto's rise, a new paradigm.
Each asset class with pros and cons,
A choice for all, which one belongs?

Weigh the risks, the power, the gains,
Against surveillance and fiscal chains.
Choose wisely, for the future's near,
A financial fortress to hold dear.

CHAPTER 9: Choosing Your Financial Fortress: Gold, Silver, Crypto, and the Battle Against CBDCs

As we arrive at the conclusion of this enlightening exploration, it's clear that the global financial terrain is in the throes of rapid transformation. The conventional model of fiat currency is on the verge of collapse, echoing the fate of its historical counterparts. In parallel, Central Bank Digital Currencies (CBDCs) — a gateway to global, digital tyranny are gaining traction. Estimates suggest that by the year's end, CBDCs will be in use by over a billion people worldwide. Leading nations, including the United States, have conducted successful trial runs of their own versions, paving the way for the imminent, broad-scale deployment of CBDCs.

In this current climate, it's never been more essential to consciously sever ties with the faltering fiat system and transition into self-custody assets like cryptocurrency, gold, and silver. This final chapter juxtaposes these alternative assets against the backdrop of waning fiat currencies and the impending ascendance of CBDCs — unless significant action is taken to halt their proliferation.

By gaining an in-depth understanding of each asset's unique attributes and seizing control of our financial destiny, we can safeguard our wealth, uphold our privacy, and push back against the creeping centralization of power that poses a direct threat to our fundamental liberties. The call to action is urgent, and the case for doing so has never been stronger.

Why This Chapter Matters

Comparing and contrasting assets like cryptocurrencies, gold, silver, and CBDCs empowers us to make wise choices aligned with our values, goals, and risk tolerance. Gaining a holistic understanding of the pros, cons and tradeoffs of each option provides a framework for carefully crafting an investment strategy. Weighing each asset's attributes against the backdrop of waning fiat currencies and the threat of CBDCs enables us to select the most suitable assets for our financial fortress. Making informed decisions based on evidence and logic helps us reclaim power over our finances and take responsibility for securing them.

Dimension	Gold	Silver	Crypto (Bitcoin and others)	Fiat Currency	CBDC
Portability	Low	Low	High	High	High
Durability	High	High	High	Low	High
Divisibility	Low	Low	High	High	High
Recognizability	High	High	Medium	High	High
Liquidity	High	High	High	High	High
Store of Value	High	High	Medium	Low	Low
Volatility	Low	Low	High	Low	Low
Censorable	Low	Low	Low	High	High
Fixed Supply	Yes	Yes	Yes	No	No
Total Financial Surveillance	Low	Low	Low	High	Very High
Centralization of Power	Low	Low	Low	High	Very High
Programmable Money Restrictions	No	No	No	Yes	Yes
Negative Interest Rates	No	No	Now	Yes	Yes
Exclusion of Vulnerable Groups	Low	Low	Medium	Low	High
Cybersecurity Risks	Low	Low	Medium	Low	Medium
Systemic Failures	Low	Low	Low	Medium	Medium

1. Portability: The ease with which an asset can be carried and transported. For example, digital assets like Bitcoin and CBDCs are highly portable because they can be easily moved and stored electronically. Gold and silver, on the other hand, are less portable due to their physical weight and the need for secure storage.

2. Durability: The ability of an asset to withstand wear, damage, or decay over time. Gold and silver are highly durable as they don't corrode or degrade. Fiat currency, however, can wear out or become damaged. Digital assets like Bitcoin and CBDCs have high durability since they exist electronically, making them immune to physical wear.

3. Divisibility: The extent to which an asset can be divided into smaller units without losing value. Digital assets like Bitcoin and CBDCs are highly divisible, allowing for transactions of very small amounts. Gold and silver, while divisible, can be more challenging to divide into smaller units, especially in everyday transactions.

4. Recognizability: The ease with which an asset can be identified and accepted by others. Gold and silver are widely recognizable due to their long history as stores of value. Fiat currency is also highly recognizable. Bitcoin's recognizability is growing but still limited compared to traditional assets, while a dystopian CBDC would likely have high recognizability within its jurisdiction.

5. Liquidity: The ease with which an asset can be converted into cash or other assets without affecting its value. Gold, silver, and fiat currency generally have high liquidity due to their widespread acceptance. Bitcoin's liquidity is improving but may still face limitations, while a CBDC would likely be highly liquid within its jurisdiction.

6. Store of Value: The ability of an asset to maintain its value over time without significant depreciation. Gold and silver have historically served as stores of value, while fiat currencies can lose value due to inflation. Bitcoin's store of value is debated due to its volatility, and a dystopian CBDC may not be a reliable store of value if subject to negative interest rates or arbitrary restrictions.

7. Volatility: The degree of fluctuation in an asset's value. Bitcoin is known for its high volatility, while gold and silver have lower volatility. Fiat currencies and CBDCs typically exhibit low volatility, but exceptions may occur during economic crises or extreme events.

8. Censorable: The extent to which transactions involving an asset can be controlled, monitored, or blocked by a central authority. Bitcoin and self-custody gold and silver have low censorship risk, while fiat currency and CBDCs can be censored or restricted by governments or financial institutions.

9. Fixed Supply: Whether the total quantity of an asset is limited or predetermined. Gold and silver have limited supply, while Bitcoin has a fixed supply of 21 million coins. Fiat currency and CBDCs can be created at the discretion of central banks, leading to potential inflation.

10. Total Financial Surveillance: The degree to which financial transactions and holdings can be monitored and tracked. Bitcoin and self-custody gold and silver offer relative privacy, while fiat currency transactions through banks are more

easily traceable. A dystopian CBDC would enable extensive surveillance by the central authority.

11. Centralization of Power: The extent to which control over an asset is concentrated in the hands of a few entities. Gold and silver ownership and Bitcoin's decentralized network resist centralization. Fiat currencies and CBDCs, however, are controlled by central banks and governments, concentrating power in their hands.

12. Programmable Money Restrictions: The ability to impose rules and limitations on the use of an asset through technological means. Bitcoin and self-custody gold and silver do not have programmable restrictions, while fiat currency can be subject to capital controls. A dystopian CBDC would likely have extensive programmable restrictions, allowing the central authority to control and limit its use based on various criteria.

13. Negative Interest Rates: The possibility of having an asset's value decrease over time due to negative interest rates imposed by a central authority. Gold and silver are not subject to negative interest rates. Bitcoin, being decentralized, is also immune to such rates. However, fiat currencies and CBDCs can be subject to negative interest rates set by central banks, eroding their value over time.

14. Exclusion of Vulnerable Groups: The likelihood of certain groups being excluded from access to an asset due to economic, technological, or regulatory barriers. Gold and silver, as well as

fiat currency, have relatively low exclusion risk, as they are widely accessible. Bitcoin's exclusion risk is medium, as it requires internet access and some technical knowledge. A dystopian CBDC could have a high exclusion risk if it's used to enforce social or political objectives, potentially barring certain groups from access.

15. Cybersecurity Risks: The potential for an asset to be compromised or stolen through digital means. Gold and silver, being physical assets, have low cybersecurity risks. Bitcoin, as a digital asset, is subject to cybersecurity risks, although its decentralized nature helps mitigate some of these risks. Fiat currency has low cybersecurity risks in its physical form, but electronic transactions are exposed to risks. A dystopian CBDC would also be subject to cybersecurity risks, as it exists entirely in digital form.

16. Systemic Failures: The susceptibility of an asset to widespread disruptions or failures due to inherent weaknesses or external factors. Gold and silver are less prone to systemic failures due to their physical nature and decentralized ownership. Bitcoin's decentralized network also reduces its susceptibility to systemic failures. Fiat currency and CBDCs, being centrally controlled, may be more vulnerable to systemic failures caused by mismanagement, economic crises, or other factors. A dystopian CBDC could be at higher risk due to its centralized control and potential for misuse.

In summary, self-custody gold and silver offer advantages in durability, recognizability, store of value, and resistance to censorship and centralization.

Cryptocurrencies like Bitcoin provide portability, divisibility, and a fixed supply but has higher volatility and cybersecurity risks. Fiat currency is highly recognizable and liquid but may lose value due to inflation and is subject to censorship. A dystopian CBDC would have high surveillance and programmable restrictions, centralization of power, and could potentially exclude vulnerable groups.

As we progress to the subsequent two chapters, we'll shift our focus from the conceptual to the actionable. In Chapter 10, we'll guide you on how to procure, manage, and integrate cryptocurrency into your everyday life. Following that, Chapter 11 will provide insights on acquiring and maintaining self-custody gold and silver. Get ready to apply what you've learned in a practical context!

Key Takeaways from Chapter 9:

- Gold and silver, when self-custodied, bring forth advantages such as durability, recognizability, proven store of value, and resistance against censorship and centralized control. These timeless assets offer stability amidst financial turbulence.
- Bitcoin and other select cryptocurrencies, on the other hand, offer unique benefits such as portability, divisibility, and a capped supply. However, it also comes with challenges, including higher volatility and potential cybersecurity threats. Nonetheless, it's a pioneering asset in the world of digital currencies.
- Fiat currency, while highly recognizable and liquid, carries the risk of devaluation due to

inflation and is susceptible to censorship. It's a system that has flaws intrinsic to its design and operation.

- On the extreme end of the spectrum, a dystopian CBDC could come with invasive surveillance capabilities and programmable restrictions, resulting in an alarming consolidation of power. It might also potentially exclude certain groups, adding to social inequalities. This scenario illustrates the potential dangers of unchecked digital currency systems.

Artwork:

Unlocking the Power of Cryptocurrency: A Practical
Guide

In a world of digital gold and silver,
We find ourselves seeking to uncover,
The secrets of wallets, exchanges, and more,
Cryptocurrency, we are eager to explore.

Step by step, we learn, and we grow,
Empowered by the knowledge we bestow,
A world enlightened by crypto's embrace,
As we navigate this exciting new space.

Chapter 10: Unlocking the Power of Cryptocurrency: A Practical Guide

As we journey into the riveting domain of cryptocurrencies in this chapter, our goal is to equip you with the critical tools needed to escape the restrictions of traditional fiat currencies and the looming dystopian future posed by CBDCs. Building on the groundwork established in Chapter 6 — where we unraveled the fundamentals of cryptocurrencies, assessed their potential as alternatives to fiat or CBDCs, cautioned against the traps of centralized exchanges, emphasized the importance of self-custody for your crypto assets, and highlighted ongoing governmental efforts to curb crypto adoption — we now turn our attention towards practical strategies for incorporating cryptocurrencies into your daily life.

In this chapter, we'll provide a broad overview of the available self-custody crypto wallets, focusing specifically on the Exodus wallet. As a participant in the crypto ecosystem since 2012 and living solely on crypto since 2019, I've assisted hundreds of individuals on their crypto journeys. I've repeatedly seen the unfortunate consequences of neglecting my advice, especially regarding keeping crypto on exchanges, which can sometimes lead to a complete loss of assets.

Drawing from my first-hand experience and comprehensive research, the tools outlined below will enable you to obtain self-custody crypto (BTC, RVN, BCH, BSV, and LTC) and provide you with the means to pay your mortgage, use a debit card, buy gift cards, and pay your cell phone bill using cryptocurrencies.

While there's a plethora of solutions available, our aim here is to simplify the process, allowing you to set up and start using crypto in less than 20 minutes by following these uncomplicated steps. Please remember that this guide isn't exhaustive, and there may be other ways to accomplish the same objectives. However, we've chosen to highlight the most accessible and user-friendly approach in this book.

As the tech landscape continues to evolve, we encourage you to stay informed about the latest advancements by visiting our website at http://www.daylightnetwork.com. Embrace the future of finance, take control of your assets, and harness the power of cryptocurrencies.

Why This Chapter Matters

By adhering to practical guides for using and safeguarding self-custody cryptocurrencies, we can take decisive steps to fortify our financial autonomy. Utilizing insights into procuring and storing these digital assets through easy-to-follow, step-by-step instructions, even those with limited technical knowledge are empowered to join the cryptocurrency revolution. Experiencing firsthand the potential of these options to replace fiat currency fosters faith in their long-term viability. As we take ownership of our financial futures through cryptocurrencies, we nurture qualities of independence, accountability, and resilience, all of which are vital for navigating the labyrinth of an uncertain economic future.

Overview of crypto wallet types

There are three main categories of self-custody crypto wallets: software wallets, hardware wallets, and paper wallets.

Software wallets are applications that can be downloaded onto your computer or mobile device. They are free to use and easy to set up, making them a great option for beginners. Examples of software wallets include Exodus, Atomic Wallet, and Electrum.

Hardware wallets are physical devices that store your private keys offline. They offer the highest level of security for your crypto assets, but they come with a higher price tag. Hardware wallets are ideal for those who plan to hold large amounts of crypto for an extended period. Examples of hardware wallets include Ledger Nano S, Trezor, and KeepKey.

Paper wallets are a low-tech option for storing crypto. They involve printing out your private key and public address onto a piece of paper, which can be stored in a safe or other secure location. Paper wallets are a good option for those who want to store crypto offline without investing in a hardware wallet. Examples of paper wallets include Bitaddress.org and WalletGenerator.net.

Using Exodus wallet to store your crypto in one wallet

For this guide, we will focus on the software wallet Exodus. With one Exodus wallet you can store your Bitcoin (BTC), Ravencoin (RVN), Bitcoin Cash (BCH), Bitcoin SV (BSV), and Litecoin (LTC). To download and use Exodus, follow these simple steps:

1. Go to the Exodus website (https://www.exodus.com/) and download the wallet for your operating system.
2. Install and launch the wallet.
3. Now that you have the wallet, you will want to make sure to secure it. Click on "Backup" to create a strong password AND write it down in a safe place:
   a. Minimum of 16 characters
   b. Combination of lower- and upper-case letters
   c. Numbers
   d. Symbols
      Do not use common names or information available about you on social media, passwords from other sites, or easily guessed passwords.
4. Write down the 12-word recovery phrase and keep in a safe place. If you lose this, you lose your crypto- there is no way to reset your password if you forget it without the recovery phrase.
   a. Write it on a piece of paper/notebook and keep secret.
   b. DO NOT take screenshots or store in any electronic form especially a cloud service like gmail/DropBox/Evernote etc.

    c. Make sure the words are spelled correctly and in the correct order.

5. Return to the Exodus homepage and select the 'Fiat Onramp' to BUY cryptocurrency (it is an icon with a dollar sign in it
    a. Cryptocurrency can be purchased/sold in fractions of a 'coin'.
6. Choose a payment method and follow the prompts to complete the purchase.
7. Your purchased cryptocurrency will appear in your Exodus wallet.
8. By following these steps, readers can easily set up a self-custody crypto wallet and purchase their first cryptocurrency in under 15 minutes.

Using Changenow.io to convert some of your BTC, BCH, and LTC to RVN and BSV

Note: While you can store all five of the crypto on the exodus wallet, you can currently only purchase BTC, BCH, and LTC through the Exodus wallet directly. There is an easy solution to converting some of your BTC, BCH, and LTC to RVN or BSV using a service called ChangeNow.io. I recommend that you use either BCH or LTC to convert to RVN and BSV because the fees are significantly lower. Here are the steps to convert your BTC, BCH, and LTC to RVN and BSV:

- Step 1: Set up a cryptocurrency wallet
  1. Before you start, you need a wallet to store your purchased RVN or BSV. Download and install the Exodus wallet as per the previous instructions and follow the wallet's instructions to set up an account. Make sure to back up your wallet's recovery phrase and keep it in a safe place.

- Step 2: Access ChangeNow.io
  1. Visit ChangeNow.io using your internet browser. ChangeNow.io is a user-friendly platform that allows you to convert one cryptocurrency quickly and easily to another without the need for an account.
- Step 3: Choose your cryptocurrencies
  1. On the ChangeNow.io homepage, you'll see two dropdown menus: "You send" and "You get." In the "You send" dropdown menu, select the cryptocurrency you want to convert (BTC, BCH, or LTC). In the "You get" dropdown menu, choose the cryptocurrency you want to receive (RVN or BSV).
- Step 4: Enter the amount to exchange Input the amount of BTC, BCH, or LTC you want to convert.
  1. ChangeNow.io will automatically calculate the estimated amount of RVN or BSV you will receive based on the current exchange rate. Note that the final amount may vary slightly due to market fluctuations.
- Step 5: Provide your wallet address
  1. To receive your converted RVN or BSV, you need to provide your wallet's receiving address. Open your wallet app, find the "Receive" or "Request" option, and copy your RVN or BSV wallet address. Paste the copied address into the "Recipient address" field on ChangeNow.io.
- Step 6: Confirm transaction details
  1. Review the transaction details, including the amount of crypto to be exchanged and

the recipient address. Make sure everything is correct, then click "Next" to proceed.

- Step 7: Send your crypto to ChangeNow.io
  1. ChangeNow.io will now provide you with a unique deposit address. Copy this address and go to your BTC, BCH, or LTC wallet. Send the specified amount of crypto to the provided deposit address.
- Step 8: Wait for the exchange to complete
  1. Once ChangeNow.io receives your deposit, they will begin the conversion process. This usually takes a few minutes but may take longer depending on network congestion. You can monitor the progress of your transaction on the ChangeNow.io website.
- Step 9: Receive your RVN or BSV
  1. When the exchange is complete, ChangeNow.io will send the converted RVN or BSV to your provided wallet address. Check your wallet to confirm that you have received the funds.

Using Changenow.io in conjunction with the Exodus wallet will allow you to have all five of these coins safely in your own custody.

How you can pay your mortgage and convert your crypto to cash on a pre-paid debit card using BitPay

Now that you have self-custody crypto, you are probably wondering how you can use crypto to pay your bills. Just as there are many different wallets you could use; I recommend what I have personally found to be the most reliable option in the marketplace to date. The market moves quickly so you will want to stay on top of the different vendors that are available. I have found for paying bills, the best option out there is to use a service called BitPay. Using BitPay, you can pay your mortgage directly through their service and can also obtain a BitPay pre-paid debit card which you can use to convert your crypto to fiat when you need to pay for things with cash. You can use your BitPay debit card anywhere you can use any other debit card and can even use it to take cash of out ATMs.

In this guide, we will provide simple, step-by-step instructions for creating a BitPay account and using it to pay your mortgage and fund a debit card.

Step 1: Create a BitPay account
1. Visit the BitPay website (https://bitpay.com/) using your preferred internet browser.
2. Click on the "Sign Up" button located in the upper-right corner of the homepage.
3. Fill in the required information, including your email address and a secure password, then click "Sign Up."
4. Check your email for a verification message from BitPay. Click on the link provided in the email to verify your account.
5. Once your email is verified, log in to your BitPay account.

Step 2: Pay your mortgage using BitPay
Note: This step assumes that your mortgage provider accepts BitPay as a payment method.

1. Contact your mortgage provider and request instructions for making a payment using BitPay. They should provide you with a payment link or a QR code.
2. Log in to your BitPay account.

3. If you received a payment link, click on it, and you will be redirected to the BitPay payment portal. If you have a QR code, visit the "Pay" section in your BitPay account, and use the QR code scanner to scan the code.
4. Choose the cryptocurrency you want to use for payment (e.g., Bitcoin or another crypto).
5. Confirm the payment details, including the mortgage payment amount and the recipient address, then click "Confirm."
6. BitPay will generate a transaction invoice. Use your cryptocurrency wallet to send the required amount to the displayed address or scan the QR code provided within the specified time limit.
7. Once the transaction is confirmed on the blockchain, BitPay will process the payment, and your mortgage provider will receive the funds.

Step 3: Fund a debit card using BitPay
Note: This step assumes that you have a crypto-compatible debit card. UPDATE: BitPay is in the process of selecting a new bank to handle their debit card program and will be suspending this feature for the time being. The new program is expected in 2024.
1. Log in to your BitPay account.
2. Visit the "Pay" section and click on the "Fund a Debit Card" option.
3. Enter the required information, including the debit card number, the amount you want to load, and the cryptocurrency you wish to use for funding (e.g., Bitcoin or another crypto).
4. Review the transaction details and click "Confirm."
5. BitPay will generate a transaction invoice. Use your cryptocurrency wallet to send the required amount to the displayed address or scan the QR code provided within the specified time limit.

6. Once the transaction is confirmed on the blockchain, BitPay will process the payment, and the funds will be loaded onto your debit card.

By following these simple steps, you can create a BitPay account, pay your mortgage with crypto, and fund a debit card. This guide aims to help users with limited technical knowledge to navigate BitPay's platform and enjoy the convenience and flexibility of using cryptocurrencies for everyday transactions.

Using Bitrefill to buy gift cards, and pay your mobile phone bill with crypto

Bitrefill is a platform that allows users to purchase various gift cards, mobile top-ups, and vouchers with cryptocurrencies. This guide provides easy-to-understand instructions for using Bitrefill, even if you have limited technical knowledge.

Step 1: Create a Bitrefill account
1. Visit the Bitrefill website (https://www.bitrefill.com/) using your preferred internet browser.
2. Click on the "Sign Up" button located in the upper-right corner of the homepage.
3. You can sign up with your email address or by using your Google, Facebook, or Twitter account. Choose your preferred method and follow the prompts to complete the registration process.
4. If you signed up with an email address, check your email for a verification message from Bitrefill. Click on the link provided in the email to verify your account.
5. Once your email is verified, log in to your Bitrefill account.

Step 2: Browse products and add them to your cart
1. Navigate through the categories displayed on the Bitrefill homepage or use the search bar to find the product you want to purchase.
2. Once you find the product, click on it to view more details.
3. Select the desired denomination or value for the product (if applicable).
4. Click on the "Add to Cart" button to add the product to your shopping cart.
5. You can continue browsing and adding more products to your cart or proceed to checkout by clicking on the shopping cart icon in the upper-right corner.

Step 3: Checkout and choose your cryptocurrency for payment
1. Review the items in your shopping cart and click on the "Proceed to Checkout" button when you are ready to complete your purchase.
2. Enter any necessary information, such as your email address or phone number (depending on the product you are purchasing).
3. Select the cryptocurrency you want to use for payment (e.g., Bitcoin or another crypto).
4. Click on the "Continue to Payment" button.

Step 4: Complete the payment with your cryptocurrency wallet
1. Bitrefill will display a payment invoice with the cryptocurrency amount, the recipient address, and a QR code.
2. Open your cryptocurrency wallet and choose the "Send" or "Pay" option (the specific wording may vary depending on the wallet).
3. Enter the recipient address and the payment amount manually, or scan the QR code provided by Bitrefill to autofill the required information.

4. Double-check the payment details, ensuring the recipient address and amount are correct, then confirm the transaction.
5. Once the transaction is confirmed on the blockchain, Bitrefill will process the payment and send you the purchased product (e.g., a gift card code, mobile top-up, or voucher) via email or directly to your account.

By leveraging the strengths of the Exodus wallet, Changenow.io, BitPay, and Bitrefill, you are not just securing self-custody of your own crypto, but also gaining the capacity to manage all your bills and even withdraw cash from ATMs when necessary. This powerful combination propels you towards complete financial autonomy.

Key Takeaways from Chapter 10:

• By adhering to practical guides for using and safeguarding self-custody cryptocurrencies, we are able to take decisive steps to fortify our financial autonomy.
• Utilizing insights into procuring and storing these digital assets through easy-to-follow, step-by-step instructions, even those with limited technical knowledge are empowered to join the cryptocurrency revolution.
• Experiencing firsthand the potential of these options to replace fiat currency fosters faith in their long-term viability.
• As we take ownership of our financial futures through cryptocurrencies, we nurture qualities of independence, accountability, and resilience.

Artwork:

"The desire of gold is not for gold. It is for the means of freedom and benefit." - Ralph Waldo Emerson

A world of gold, in our hands to hold,
A tale of value, a story untold.
Seek wisdom in this guide we share,
To buy, secure, and show you care.

Unlock the secrets, the criteria, and choice,
In golden self-custody, let us rejoice.
Through styles, providers, and tips to secure,
Find peace and power, in gold's allure.

Chapter 11: A Practical Guide to Self-Custody Gold and Silver

In Chapters 7 and 8, we embarked on a captivating journey through the ages, tracing the history and significance of gold and silver. We explored their enduring roles as mediums of exchange, witnessed their debasement, and observed how they've weathered economic storms as steady stores of value. We also shed light on various forms of market malfeasance targeting these precious metals, underscoring the imperative need for self-custody.

Now, it's time to shift gears from theory to practice. In this chapter, we aim to equip you with practical insights on how to procure and manage your self-custody gold and silver. As the landscape of precious metals is ever evolving, we advise you to keep an eye on our website, http://www.daylightnetwork.net, for the most up-to-date information. Embark on this new chapter of your financial journey with confidence, knowing you're taking control of your wealth in the most secure way possible.

Why This Chapter Matters

Adopting practical guides for procuring and securing self-custody gold and silver enables us to reinforce our financial sovereignty. Implementing insights into acquiring and storing these precious metals, guided by straightforward, step-by-step instructions, equips us to secure our wealth in these time-tested assets even without extensive prior knowledge. Observing the enduring ability of gold and silver to serve as an alternative to fiat currency instills confidence in their long-term sustainability. As we take responsibility for our finances through gold and silver, we foster a sense of independence, accountability, and resilience, crucial for maneuvering through an unpredictable economic landscape.

Top 10 criteria to use when buying self-custody gold and silver

As you venture into the realm of self-custody gold and silver, it's vital to arm yourself with knowledge and make informed decisions. Here are the top 10 factors you should bear in mind to ensure you're making sound investments:

1. Purity: The precious metals you acquire should be of high purity — typically .999 or .9999 fine gold or silver. This guarantees that you're securing the most value from your investment. While we'll be recommending reputable national dealers to source your gold and silver, if you decide to explore local options or find yourself in a situation that demands it, be aware of various

techniques to test the purity of precious metals, including acid test kits and electronic gold testers.

2. Weight: Both gold and silver are typically sold in varying weights — grams, ounces, or kilos. Select a weight that aligns with your financial capabilities and investment objectives.

3. Reputable Dealer: Always source your precious metals from trustworthy dealers with a proven track record. This will significantly mitigate the risk of encountering fraud or counterfeit metals.

4. Recognizable Brands: Choose gold and silver products from widely recognized mints or manufacturers. These are more readily accepted and traded in the market.

5. Competitive Pricing: Don't settle for the first price you see. Compare rates across various dealers to ensure you're getting the best value for your money.

6. Secure Packaging: Your precious metals should arrive in secure packaging to safeguard them from potential damage during transit and storage.

7. Liquidity: Opt for gold and silver products that have high liquidity in the market. This ensures you can swiftly convert your investment into cash when needed.

8. Certificates of Authenticity: Always demand a certificate of authenticity when purchasing gold or silver. This document verifies the purity, weight, and origin of your precious metals.

9. Storage Options: Consider your storage options for your gold and silver, such as a home safe or a professional storage facility. Don't forget to factor in any related costs.

10. Legal Considerations: Educate yourself on any legal stipulations or restrictions associated with gold and silver ownership in your location,

including reporting obligations or tax implications.

By keeping these tenets at the forefront of your decision-making process, you'll be well-equipped to navigate the world of self-custody gold and silver.

Three Types of Self-custody gold and silver options

As you venture into self-custody precious metals, it's essential to understand the categories of self-custody for gold and silver. It's highly recommended that you maintain direct control or access to your metals. As historical instances like the 1930s gold confiscation by President FDR show, governments tend to target centralized locations. Thus, keeping your precious metals in a bank safety deposit box is not the best idea.

My advice leans towards keeping physical bullion within your personal reach. However, I present to you three distinct types of self-custody options for your gold and silver for a well-rounded perspective. Always remember that the ultimate goal is to ensure the safety and accessibility of your precious metals.

Self-Custody Option	Accessibility	Security	Cost	Complexity	Privacy	Mobility	Ease of Confiscation
Physical Bullion	High	Med	High	Low	High	Low	Med
Allocated & Segregated Storage	Med	High	Moderate	Med	Med	Low	High
P2P Gold Platforms	High	Med	Low	Med	Med	High	Low

- Physical Bullion: This option involves buying physical gold and silver in the form of coins or bars and holding them in your personal care. This approach grants you direct control over your precious metals, eliminating the need for third-party involvement and any associated risks.
- Allocated and Segregated Storage: This strategy involves buying physical gold and silver and storing them in a third-party vault or facility. With allocated storage, your precious metals are stored separately from those of other clients. Segregated storage ensures that your gold and silver are not just stored separately, but are also easily identifiable as your property. Although this option provides indirect control over your metals, it comes with enhanced security measures.
- Peer-to-Peer (P2P) Precious Metal Platforms: This approach entails purchasing digital representations of physical gold and silver through peer-to-peer platforms. These digital assets correspond to physical gold and silver held by a third-party custodian. While this option provides indirect control over your metals, it eliminates the need for physical storage, along with the associated costs and risks.

Popular Denominations and Styles of Gold:

As you venture into the domain of gold and silver investing, it's vital to grasp the array of choices at your disposal regarding self-custody and denominations. To aid you in making an enlightened choice, we've designed a detailed table that outlines the primary characteristics of popular gold and silver denominations and styles. This table will function as a helpful guide to assist you in selecting the gold and silver investment that most harmoniously matches your preferences, financial aspirations, and level of risk acceptance.

By recognizing the unique attributes of each gold and silver denomination and style, you can confidently establish a diverse and secure investment portfolio. We encourage you to take some time to peruse this table and gain a deeper understanding of the gold and silver investment landscape; this could be the key to unlocking your financial prosperity.

Here are popular denominations/styles for gold.

Denomination/Style	Description
1-100 gram increments	Popular among individual investors, easily divisible
1 oz gold coin	Popular among individual investors, commonly minted by government mints
1 kilogram gold bar	Typically preferred by institutional investors and high net worth individuals
American Eagle	Popular gold coin produced by the US Mint
Canadian Maple Leaf	Popular gold coin produced by the Royal Canadian Mint
South African Krugerrand	Popular gold coin produced by the South African Mint

Here are popular denominations/styles for silver:

Denomination/Style	Description
1 oz silver coin	Popular among individual investors, commonly minted by government mints
1 kilogram silver bar	Typically preferred by

Denomination/Style	Description
	institutional investors and high net worth individuals
American Silver Eagle	Popular silver coin produced by the US Mint
Canadian Silver Maple Leaf	Popular silver coin produced by the Royal Canadian Mint
Australian Silver Kangaroo	Popular silver coin produced by the Perth Mint

Top 10 National Gold and Silver Providers:

When it comes to investing in precious metals, choosing a reliable and reputable vendor is crucial for a seamless and secure experience. We understand that navigating through numerous options can be overwhelming, which is why we have compiled a comprehensive table comparing the top precious metal vendors across key criteria such as reputation, customer service, pricing, security, delivery, minimum order size, and contact information. This table is designed to help you make an informed decision by comparing the strengths and weaknesses of each vendor, ultimately enabling you to invest with confidence. By taking the time to understand the differences between these vendors, you can select the one that best meets your investment needs and ensures a smooth and secure precious metals purchasing experience.

Vendor	Reputation	Customer Service	Pricing	Security	Delivery	Minimum Order Size	Contact Info
APMEX	9	8	7	8	8	$1,500	www.apmex.com
JM Bullion	9	7	8	7	8	$100	www.jmbullion.com
Kitco	8	8	7	8	7	$500	www.kitco.com
Provident Metals	8	7	8	7	7	$150	www.providentmetals.com
SD Bullion	8	7	8	7	7	$100	www.sdbullion.com
BGASC	7	7	8	7	7	$100	www.bgasc.com
Money Metals	7	7	8	7	7	$100	www.moneymetals.com
Gainesville Coins	7	7	7	7	7	$100	www.gainesvillecoins.com
Texas Precious Metals	7	7	7	7	7	$1,000	www.texmetals.com
Golden Eagle Coins	7	6	7	7	7	$100	www.goldeneaglecoin.com

How to manage and secure your self-custody gold and silver

Safeguarding your valuable gold and silver investment is of paramount significance, and being familiar with the best strategies for protecting your assets is key to guaranteeing their security. That's why we've gathered a list of vital tips to help you confidently store and manage your gold and silver holdings. By adhering to these guidelines, you'll not only have peace of mind knowing your assets are safe, but also be prepared to tackle any unexpected situations. Take the time to study these essential storage tips and learn how to aptly safeguard your valuable gold and silver investments.

- Choose a secure and discreet location for storage: Your storage location should offer both security and discretion. The fewer people who know about your holdings, the better.

- Keep a detailed inventory: Maintain an accurate record of your holdings, detailing the type of metal (gold or silver), weight, and purity. This will help you monitor your assets and spot any discrepancies.
- Invest in a top-tier safe or vault: If you opt for home storage, ensure you invest in a high-quality safe or vault specifically designed for safeguarding valuables.
- Insure your holdings: Consider taking out an insurance policy on your gold and silver to cover potential theft or damage. Many insurance providers offer policies tailored for precious metals.
- Avoid locations prone to natural disasters: If your region is susceptible to natural disasters like floods or earthquakes, choose a storage location less likely to sustain damage.
- Maintain discretion: Exercise caution when discussing your gold and silver holdings, especially with those who might not have your best interests at heart.
- Regularly inspect your storage location: Make routine checks of your storage area to ensure your assets are undisturbed and secure.

Key Takeaways from Chapter 11:

- Embracing user-friendly guides for sourcing and securing self-custody gold and silver empowers us to bolster our financial independence.
- Applying learned strategies for obtaining and safeguarding these precious metals, guided by uncomplicated, step-by-step directions, prepares

us to protect our wealth in these long-standing assets, regardless of our initial expertise.

- Witnessing the continued capacity of gold and silver to act as a viable alternative to fiat currency solidifies our trust in their lasting viability.
- As we shoulder the responsibility of managing our finances through gold and silver, we cultivate a spirit of self-reliance, responsibility, and resilience in the face of economic uncertainties.

Artwork:

"The future is not some place we are going to, but one we are creating. The paths are not to be found, but made. And the activity of making them, changes both the maker and the destination." - John Schaar

My friends, we have traversed a winding path,
From fiat's failings to crypto's aftermath.
As gov't control encroaches our lives,
Self-custody shines, freedom survives.

Now dawns a new day, our journey's end,
But this first step, our tale, it doth lend
New purpose and hope for all who seek
To reclaim powers, long since week.

This fight is but one against tyranny's stride,
While faith, truth and love stay by our side.
Though fiat may fall, and CBDCs rise,
Together we stand, the phoenix that flies.

Chapter 12: Taking Action Towards Financial Freedom

As we reach the conclusion of this book, let's reflect on the knowledge we've gained and the measures we can take to ensure our financial independence.

Why This Chapter Matters

Reflecting on the pivotal lessons and imperative actions suggested in this book reaffirms our commitment to secure our financial independence. Consolidating these key insights strengthens our understanding and conviction. Revisiting the advised courses of action offers us a blueprint to put our newfound knowledge into practice. Recognizing that we are part of a broader movement advocating for individual sovereignty fosters a sense of hope, unity, and bravery. Embracing our responsibility to disseminate this knowledge amplifies our potential for positive influence. Cherishing the belief that love and wisdom invariably triumph over forces of control fuels our inspiration as we embark on this dignified journey towards autonomy.

Here are the key takeaways from our exploration:

- Fiat currencies, by nature, are unstable and prone to failure, which underlines the necessity to diversify into alternative assets.
- The advent of Central Bank Digital Currencies (CBDCs) poses a threat to basic freedoms and privacy, making it essential to embrace self-custody crypto, gold, and silver to prevent total control.
- Institutions like the UN, WEF, World Bank, IMF, and BIS are promoting a centralized agenda, which further underscores the need for decentralization.
- History has demonstrated that self-custody assets like crypto, gold, and silver have maintained value through economic turbulence, indicating that they continue to be reliable stores of wealth.
- Technologies supporting self-custody are readily accessible, empowering individuals to regain control of their financial health amidst growing threats.

Armed with this understanding, here are the vital steps you can undertake to fortify your financial independence:

1. Devise a strategy: Determine the share of your wealth you wish to allocate to diverse assets

based on your risk tolerance, objectives, and inclinations. Remember, responsible diversification is key.

2. Invest judiciously: Opt for reputable brands when buying self-custody gold and silver and select cryptocurrencies that offer everyday utility and long-term value. Steer clear of centralized exchanges.

3. Store assets securely: Set up your own self-custody wallets, invest in a robust physical safe or choose a reliable storage provider. Exercise complete ownership.

4. Stay abreast of developments: Remain informed about shifts in policy, technology, and the macroeconomic environment that could influence your finances and freedoms. Be prepared to adapt.

5. Spread the knowledge: Enlighten those around you about the concepts discussed in this book. The broader the understanding of these issues, the more effective the solutions will be. Also, read and share THE BANK RUN MANIFESTO below.

6. Preserve optimism: Keep in mind that love, wisdom, and community will ultimately prevail over forces of control and centralization. Be a catalyst for change.

Embarking on this journey begins with taking that initial step, no matter how small. I wish you the utmost success on your path towards financial and personal sovereignty—a form of freedom that remains impervious to governmental control.

On March 31, 2023, I posted the following as a call to action to exit the banks to stop World War III, End the Fed, and halt CBDC. As of the publishing of the book, the tweet has been viewed almost 800k times and has been broadly shared.

I encourage you to view, like, and share the tweet:

https://twitter.com/AaronRDay/status/164192477112945868 9?s=20

THE BANK RUN MANIFESTO

Fellow Americans, the time has come for us to unite and take a stand against the encroaching threats of WW3, financial collapse, political persecution, censorship, and crypto bans. We must recognize that change won't come from protests or the political process. It demands our collective courage to engage in mass civil disobedience. Let us come together, boldly say NO, and take action to dismantle the corrupt system that seeks to undermine our freedom.
Welcome to the Bank Run Manifesto – a call to action for us all.

We face a grave reality: protests and the ballot box have failed to address the pressing issues of our time. As we stand on the brink of global conflict, economic ruin, and increasing control over our lives, we must unite and take matters into our own hands. Consider the following five areas of oppression:

1. Verge of WW3: Our government continues to escalate tensions with China and Russia, despite overwhelming public opposition. Voting has proven ineffective against the Deep State, and we must starve the fiat currency that fuels war.

2. Financial Collapse: The US Dollar is on the verge of collapse due to economic mismanagement, unsustainable debt, and government corruption. By embracing self-

custody crypto, gold, and silver, we can protect ourselves and demand a new, more equitable financial system.

3. Political Persecution: The recent arrest of former President Trump on hush money charges highlights the abuse of power at play. Protests have been manipulated, but a bank run sends an unmistakable message: overreach will not be tolerated.

4. Censorship: Douglass Mackey's trial for posting a meme and the proposed RESTRICT Act illustrate the erosion of our First Amendment rights. By defunding the institutions behind these attacks, we can resist the encroaching tyranny.

5. Crackdown on Cryptocurrency: Congress will not willingly relinquish its control over fiat money. By embracing crypto, gold, and silver for day-to-day commerce, we can challenge this monopoly and secure our freedom.

Our call to action is simple: participate in a bank run, exchanging your dollars for alternative assets like cryptocurrencies, gold, and silver. Then, tell three others to do the same and encourage them to spread the word to three more people. Just as the 3% of the population who fought in the American Revolution made a profound impact, so too can we transform our society through collective action.

It is time to initiate a bank run that shatters the foundations of control and reclaims our financial destiny. As we come together, undivided by the shackles of prejudice and discord, we become an indomitable force. We stand for liberty, for autonomy, and for justice.

Together, we can break free from the shackles of centralized control and forge a future that values individual sovereignty, liberty, and justice for all. Stand with us, take control of your assets, and embrace the power of the people! Let our collective action echo through history, inspiring generations to come. The time is now – join us in this vital act of civil disobedience and reclaim the destiny that belongs to each and every one of us.

Key Takeaways from Chapter 12:

- Reflecting on the pivotal lessons and imperative actions suggested in this book reaffirms our commitment to secure our financial independence.
- Consolidating these key insights strengthens our understanding and conviction.
- Revisiting the advised courses of action offers us a blueprint to put our newfound knowledge into practice.
- Recognizing that we are part of a broader movement advocating for individual sovereignty fosters a sense of hope, unity, and bravery.
- Embracing our responsibility to disseminate this knowledge amplifies our potential for positive influence.

Artwork:

References

Chapter 2 References

1. Beauchamp, Zack (2019). "China's social credit system: What you need to know about the dystopian surveillance nightmare." Vox. Retrieved from https://www.vox.com/future-perfect/2019/5/7/18528534/china-social-credit-system-explainer
2. Bostrom, Nick (2005). "A history of transhumanist thought." Journal of Evolution and Technology, 14(1), 1-25.
3. Bregman, Rutger (2020). "Universal basic income: Utopian idea could become vital safety net." The Guardian. Retrieved from https://www.theguardian.com/commentisfree/2020/apr/15/universal-basic-income-coronavirus-covid-19-safety-net
4. Cadwalladr, Carole (2018). "The Cambridge Analytica scandal changed the world – but it didn't change Facebook." The Guardian. Retrieved from https://www.theguardian.com/technology/2018/oct/21/facebook-scandal-cambridge-analytica-changed-world-paul-brislen
5. Calamur, Krishnadev (2018). "China's chilling 'social credit' blacklists." The Atlantic. Retrieved from https://www.theatlantic.com/international/archive/2018/02/china-surveillance/552203/
6. Cook, Sarah (2020). "Beijing's Global Megaphone." Freedom House. Retrieved from https://freedomhouse.org/report/special-report/2020/beijings-global-megaphone

7. Downs, Erica (2018). "Huawei: The company and the security risks explained." The Brookings Institution. Retrieved from https://www.brookings.edu/blog/order-from-chaos/2018/12/17/huawei-the-company-and-the-security-risks-explained/

8. Dyste, Richard (2017). "The surveillance state: A timeline of the National Security Agency." Time. Retrieved from https://time.com/3722150/nsa-surveillance/

9. Frier, Sarah (2019). "TikTok's owner had $7 billion in revenue for the first half." Bloomberg. Retrieved from https://www.bloomberg.com/news/articles/2019-07-29/tiktok-owner-bytedance-said-to-post-7-billion-in-first-half

10. Greenwald, Glenn (2014). "No place to hide: Edward Snowden, the NSA, and the US surveillance state." Metropolitan Books.

11. Hasson, Uri & Aday, Daniel C. (2012). "The paradox of the uncanny valley." Trends in Cognitive Sciences, 16(4), 181-182.

12. Human Rights Watch (2019). "China's Algorithms of Repression: Reverse Engineering a Xinjiang Police Mass Surveillance App." Retrieved from https://www.hrw.org/report/2019/05/01/chinas-algorithms-repression/reverse-engineering-xinjiang-police-mass

13. Kehoe, Elaine (2020). "The ethics of euthanasia." The Lancet, 395(10223), 477.

14. Kirkpatrick, David D. (2020). "As Protests Swell, U.S. Surveillance Expands." The New York Times. Retrieved from https://www.nytimes.com/2020/06/13/us/politics/george-floyd-protests-surveillance.html

15. Lyons, Kim (2020). "IRS will now require taxpayers to report payments over $600 made through Venmo, PayPal, and other apps." The Verge. Retrieved from https://www.theverge.com

16. Goldstein, D. (2022). "Canada offered to help euthanize this disabled woman." New York Post. Retrieved from https://nypost.com/2022/12/03/canada-offered-to-help-euthanize-christine-gauthier/

17. Reuters (2023). "Novak Djokovic to miss Miami Open after vaccine exemption request denied." MSN. Retrieved from https://www.msn.com/en-us/sports/tennis/novak-djokovic-to-miss-miami-open-after-vaccine-exemption-request-denied/ar-AA18MXPy

18. Kraychik, R. (2023). "Legal Experts Warn Disinformation Court Case Could Set Dangerous Precedent." Daily Caller. Retrieved from https://dailycaller.com/2023/02/13/legal-experts-disinformation-court-case-douglass-mackey/

Chapter 3 References

1. Bank for International Settlements. (2021). Central bank digital currencies: foundational principles and core features. Retrieved from https://www.bis.org/publ/othp33.pdf

2. Carstens, A. (2021). Cross-border payments: a vision for the future. Retrieved from https://www.bis.org/speeches/sp200715.htm

3. Davos Manifesto. (2020). World Economic Forum. Retrieved from https://www.weforum.org/great-reset/about

4. Gabbard, T. (2019). Stop Arming Terrorists Act. Retrieved from

https://www.congress.gov/bill/115th-congress/house-bill/608

5. Huxley, J. (1946). UNESCO: Its Purpose and Its Philosophy. Retrieved from https://unesdoc.unesco.org/ark:/48223/pf000006 1621

6. IMF. (2021). Central Bank Digital Currency: A Primer. Retrieved from https://www.imf.org/external/pubs/ft/fandd/2021/06/central-bank-digital-currency-cbdc-pilot-barbados-mottley.htm

7. Ramaswamy, V. (2021). Woke, Inc: Inside Corporate America's Social Justice Scam. Hachette Books.

8. Schwab, K. (2020). The Great Reset. World Economic Forum. Retrieved from https://www.weforum.org/agenda/2020/06/now-is-the-time-for-a-great-reset/

9. United Nations. (2015). Transforming our world: the 2030 Agenda for Sustainable Development. Retrieved from https://sdgs.un.org/2030agenda

10. United Nations. (2021). Secretary-General's Roadmap for Digital Cooperation. Retrieved from https://www.un.org/en/content/digital-cooperation-roadmap/assets/pdf/Roadmap_for_Digital_Coop eration.pdf

11. Wells, H. G. (1940). The New World Order. Secker & Warburg.

12. World Economic Forum. (2020). Central Bank Digital Currency Policy-Maker Toolkit. Retrieved from https://www.weforum.org/reports/central-bank-digital-currency-policy-maker-toolkit

13. World Economic Forum. (2020). The Future of Digital Currency. Retrieved from

https://www.weforum.org/projects/digital-currency-governance-consortium
14. World Economic Forum. (2021). Global leaders of the Fourth Industrial Revolution. Retrieved from https://www.weforum.org/communities/global-leaders-of-the-fourth-industrial-revolution
15. Yuval Harari, N. (2018). 21 Lessons for the 21st Century. Spiegel & Grau.

Chapter 4 References

1. Accenture. (n.d.). Central Bank Digital Currency (CBDC): What you need to know. https://www.accenture.com/us-en/insights/banking/central-bank-digital-currency
2. Bank for International Settlements. (2021). Ready, steady, go? Results of the third BIS survey on central bank digital currency. https://www.bis.org/publ/bppdf/bispap114.pdf
3. Bank of England. (n.d.). Central Bank Digital Currency. https://www.bankofengland.co.uk/research/digital-currencies
4. Chen, L. Y. (2021, March 31). China's Digital Yuan Comes With an Annoying but Mandatory Privacy Feature. Bloomberg. https://www.bloomberg.com/news/articles/2021-03-30/china-s-digital-yuan-comes-with-an-annoying-but-mandatory-privacy-feature
5. Computerworld. (n.d.). Central Bank Digital Currencies: What's the point? https://www.computerworld.com/news-analysis/
6. Cryptoslate. (2021). Digital Yuan: How China's Digital Currency Works. https://cryptoslate.com/chinas-fujian-province-

processes-nearly-22b-in-digital-yuan-transactions/
7. The Economist. (2021). The rise of digital currencies. https://www.economist.com/finance-and-economics/2021/02/18/the-rise-of-digital-currencies
8. Epstein, J. (n.d.). The Future of Money: Central Bank Digital Currencies. https://www.jeffreyepstein.org/CBDC
9. Executive Office of the President. (2021). Executive Order 14067—Ensuring Responsible Development of Digital Assets. https://www.presidency.ucsb.edu/documents/executive-order-14067-ensuring-responsible-development-digital-assets
10. Federal Reserve Bank of Boston. (n.d.). Project Hamilton. https://www.bostonfed.org/publications/one-time-pubs/project-hamilton-phase-1-executive-summary.aspx
11. Federal Reserve Bank of New York. (n.d.). Project Cedar. https://www.newyorkfed.org/aboutthefed/nyic/project-cedar
12. Financial Times. (2021). China's digital currency: the future of money or Orwellian control? https://www.ft.com/content/5e5d5a5b-9757-4e4b-958a-4eeb817e8127
13. Gates, B. (n.d.). The Future of Money. https://www.gatesnotes.com/Books/The-Future-of-Money
14. Icke, D. (1999). The Biggest Secret. Bridge of Love.
15. Jones, A. (2021). The Great Reset. Infowars Publishing.
16. MIT Media Lab. (n.d.). Central Bank Digital Currency Initiative.

https://www.media.mit.edu/projects/cbdc/overvie
w/
17. Mora, M. (2021, October 25). Nigeria launches
eNaira as digital currency race gathers pace. Al
Jazeera.
https://www.aljazeera.com/economy/2021/10/25/
nigeria-launches-enaira-as-digital-currency-race-
gathers-pace
18. New York Fed. (n.d.). FedNow Service.
https://www.newyorkfed.org/aboutthefed/fednow
19. Nigeria Central Bank. (2021). eNaira.
https://www.cbn.gov.ng/enaira
20. People's Bank of China. (n.d.). Digital Currency
Electronic Payment (DCEP).
http://www.pbc.gov.cn/en/3688110/3688172/ind
ex.html
21. Wired. (n.d.). China's Digital Yuan (eCNY)
Works Just Like Cash, With Surveillance.
https://www.wired.com/story/chinas-digital-
yuan-ecny-works-just-like-cash-surveillance/
22. Coingeek. (n.d.). China Digital Yuan Sees
Dismal Adoption in Hong Kong.
https://coingeek.com/china-digital-yuan-sees-
dismal-adoption-in-hong-kong/
23. Financial Times. (n.d.). China's digital currency:
the future of money or Orwellian control?
https://www.ft.com/content/7511809e-827e-
4526-81ad-ae83f405f623
24. Cointelegraph. (n.d.). Nigeria CBDC adoption
spikes as fiat currency shortage grips the nation.
https://cointelegraph.com/news/nigeria-cbdc-
adoption-spikes-as-fiat-currency-shortage-grip-
the-nation
25. Bloomberg. (n.d.). Shunned Digital Currency
Looks for Street Credibility in Nigeria.
https://www.bloomberg.com/news/articles/2022-
10-25/shunned-digital-currency-looks-for-street-

credibility-in-nigeria?leadSource=uverify%20wall
26. Decrypt. (n.d.). Inside Nigeria's Ambitious Push for a Cashless Society and eNaira. https://decrypt.co/117229/inside-nigerias-ambitious-push-of-cashless-society-and-enaira
27. Forbes. (n.d.). Nigerian Election and Naira Crisis Is Fueling Bitcoin Adoption. https://www.forbes.com/sites/abubakarnurkhalil/2023/03/01/nigerian-election-and-naira-crisis-is-fueling-bitcoin-adoption/?sh=1476976d35d4
28. Coindesk. (n.d.). Nigerians' Rejection of Their CBDC Is a Cautionary Tale for Other Countries. https://www.coindesk.com/consensus-magazine/2023/03/06/nigerians-rejection-of-their-cbdc-is-a-cautionary-tale-for-other-countries/
29. Digital Dollar Project. (n.d.). About. https://www.digitaldollarproject.org/about
30. Husch Blackwell. (n.d.). U.S. DOJ Responds to Biden Executive Order on Digital Assets. https://www.huschblackwell.com/newsandinsights/us-doj-responds-to-biden-executive-order-on-digital-assets
31. U.S. Department of the Treasury. (n.d.). The Future of Money and Payments. https://home.treasury.gov/system/files/136/Future-of-Money-and-Payments.pdf
32. U.S. Department of Commerce. (n.d.). Digital Asset Competitiveness Report. https://www.commerce.gov/sites/default/files/2022-09/Digital-Asset-Competitiveness-Report.pdf
33. Federal Reserve. (n.d.). Money and Payments. https://www.federalreserve.gov/publications/files/money-and-payments-20220120.pdf

34. Federal Reserve. (n.d.). Press Release. https://www.federalreserve.gov/newsevents/press releases/other20230315a.htm
35. White House. (n.d.). Fact Sheet. https://www.whitehouse.gov/briefing-room/statements-releases/2022/09/16/fact-sheet-white-house-releases-first-ever-comprehensive-framework-for-responsible-development-of-digital -assets/
36. BeInCrypto. (n.d.). Federal Reserve to Launch FedNow Instant Payments, CBDC to Follow? https://beincrypto.com/federal-reserve-launch-fednow-instant-payments-cbdc-follow/
37. Forbes. (n.d.). The Federal Reserve Should Drop FedNow and Any Plans to Launch a CBDC. https://www.forbes.com/sites/norbertmichel/202 2/12/15/the-federal-reserve-should-drop-fednow-and-any-plans-to-launch-a-cbdc/?sh=74d9574ffd7f
38. Reuters. (n.d.). Banking Giants, New York Fed Start 12-Week Digital Dollar Pilot. https://www.reuters.com/markets/currencies/ban king-giants-new-york-fed-start-12-week-digital-dollar-pilot-2022-11-15/
39. American Banker. (n.d.). CBDC Projects Pick Up the Pace as 2023 Kicks Off. https://www.americanbanker.com/payments/list/ cbdc-projects-pick-up-the-pace-as-2023-kicks-off
40. CoinSpeaker. (n.d.). New York Fed, CBDC, and US Banks. https://www.coinspeaker.com/new-york-fed-cbdc-us-banks/
41. New York Fed. (n.d.). Project Cedar Phase One Report. https://www.newyorkfed.org/medialibrary/media /nyic/project-cedar-phase-one-report.pdf

42. Boston Fed. (n.d.). Project Hamilton: Phase 1 Executive Summary. https://www.bostonfed.org/publications/one-time-pubs/project-hamilton-phase-1-executive-summary.aspx
43. Forbes. (n.d.). Project Hamilton: On the Report Published by the Boston Fed and MIT. https://www.forbes.com/sites/vipinbharathan/2022/02/09/project-hamilton-on-the-report-published-by-the-boston-fed-and-mit/?sh=5a2257021d83
44. Hamilton Whitepaper. (n.d.). Central Bank Digital Currency: Project Hamilton. https://static1.squarespace.com/static/59aae5e9a803bb10bedeb03e/t/61fc25f91a0df9037488eb7d/1643914745989/Hamilton.Whitepaper-2022-02-02-FINAL2.pdf

Chapter 5 References

1. Al Jazeera. (2023, January 12). El Salvador passes law on cryptocurrency transfers. Retrieved from https://www.aljazeera.com/news/2023/1/12/el-salvador-passes-law-on-cryptocurrency-transfers
2. National Bureau of Economic Research. (2022, July). El Salvador's Experiment with Bitcoin as Legal Tender. Retrieved from https://www.nber.org/digest/202207/el-salvadors-experiment-bitcoin-legal-tender
3. Reuters. (2023, February 11). IMF says El Salvador's Bitcoin risks have not materialized, should be addressed. Retrieved from https://www.reuters.com/business/finance/imf-says-el-salvadors-bitcoin-risks-have-not-materialized-should-be-addressed-2023-02-11/

4. Cointelegraph. (2022). El Salvador's Bitcoin strategy evolved with the bear market in 2022. Retrieved from https://cointelegraph.com/news/el-salvador-s-bitcoin-strategy-evolved-with-the-bear-market-in-2022

5. The Wall Street Journal. (2023). The New York Couple Behind El Salvador's Bitcoin Experiment. Retrieved from https://www.wsj.com/articles/the-new-york-couple-behind-el-salvadors-bitcoin-experiment-a94446f4

6. Cointelegraph. (2023). El Salvador removes all taxes related to tech innovation for economic growth. Retrieved from https://cointelegraph.com/news/el-salvador-removes-all-taxes-related-to-tech-innovation-for-economic-growth

7. Bernholz, P. (2003). Monetary Regimes and Inflation: History, Economic, and Political Relationships. Edward Elgar Publishing.

8. Bonner, W. (2006). Empire of Debt: The Rise of an Epic Financial Crisis. John Wiley & Sons.

9. Daly, H. E., & Farley, J. (2011). Ecological Economics: Principles and Applications. Island Press.

10. Davies, G. (2002). A History of Money: From Ancient Times to the Present Day. University of Wales Press.

11. Ferguson, N. (2008). The Ascent of Money: A Financial History of the World. Penguin Books.

12. Graeber, D. (2011). Debt: The First 5,000 Years. Melville House.

13. Icke, D. (1999). The Biggest Secret: The Book That Will Change the World. Bridge of Love.

14. Griffin, G. E. (1994). The Creature from Jekyll Island: A Second Look at the Federal Reserve. American Media.
15. Paul, R. (2009). End the Fed. Grand Central Publishing.
16. Reinhart, C. M., & Rogoff, K. S. (2009). This Time Is Different: Eight Centuries of Financial Folly. Princeton University Press.
17. Rickards, J. (2011). Currency Wars: The Making of the Next Global Crisis. Penguin Books.
18. Rothbard, M. N. (2008). The Mystery of Banking. Ludwig von Mises Institute.
19. Stiglitz, J. E. (2016). The Euro: How a Common Currency Threatens the Future of Europe. W. W. Norton & Company.
20. Taleb, N. N. (2007). The Black Swan: The Impact of the Highly Improbable. Random House.

Chapter 6 References

1. The Guardian. (2022). FTX Crypto King Sam Bankman-Fried subject of new book by Michael Lewis. Retrieved from https://www.theguardian.com/books/2022/nov/1 4/ftx-crypto-king-sam-bankman-fried-new-book-michael-lewis
2. Reuters. (2023). U.S. charges FTX's Bankman-Fried with paying $40 mln Chinese bribe. Retrieved from https://www.reuters.com/legal/ftxs-bankman-fried-charged-with-bribery-conspiracy-new-indictment-2023-03-28/
3. CBS News. (2022). Sam Bankman-Fried donated over $40 million in the 2022 election cycle. Where did it go? Retrieved from

https://www.cbsnews.com/news/ftx-sam-bankman-fried-political-donations-2022/
4. We Got This Covered. (n.d.). Every Celebrity Involved in Promoting FTX Crypto. Retrieved from https://wegotthiscovered.com/tech/every-celebrity-involved-in-promoting-ftx-crypto
5. CoinDesk. (2022). Why Is Crypto Tanking: The FTX-Binance Drama Explained. Retrieved from https://www.coindesk.com/business/2022/11/09/why-is-crypto-tanking-the-ftx-binance-drama-explained/
6. Investopedia. (n.d.). Mt. Gox. Retrieved from https://www.investopedia.com/terms/m/mt-gox.asp
7. Cointelegraph. (n.d.). Mt. Gox Creditor Saga: What Lessons has the Bitcoin Community Learned. Retrieved from https://cointelegraph.com/news/mt-gox-creditor-saga-what-lessons-has-the-bitcoin-community-learned
8. Hacker Noon. (n.d.). All Cryptocurrency Exchanges Fail for the Same Reason. Retrieved from https://hackernoon.com/all-cryptocurrency-exchanges-fail-for-the-same-reason-5ds38s8
9. Roll Call. (2023). After a year of collapses, cryptocurrency's future in the balance. Retrieved from https://rollcall.com/2023/01/04/after-a-year-of-collapses-crytocurrencys-future-in-the-balance/
10. Milk Road. (n.d.). Bankruptcies. Retrieved from https://milkroad.com/bankruptcies
11. Reuters. (2023). Cryptos String of Bankruptcies. Retrieved from https://www.reuters.com/business/finance/cryptos-string-bankruptcies-2023-01-20/
12. Cooper & Kirk. (2023). Operation Choke Point 2.0. Retrieved from

https://www.cooperkirk.com/wp-content/uploads/2023/03/Operation-Choke-Point-2.0.pdf

13. Ropes & Gray LLP. (2022). SEC v. LBRY: Examining the Implications of the SEC's Latest Victory for Crypto and Digital Asset Markets. Retrieved from https://www.ropesgray.com/en/newsroom/alerts/2022/december/sec-lbry-examining-the-implications-of-the-secs-latest-victory-for-crypto-and-digital-asset-markets

14. Decrypt. (2022). LBRY Loses SEC Case, 'Dangerous Precedent' for Crypto. Retrieved from https://decrypt.co/113754/lbry

15. Forbes. (2023). Crypto Crackdown: Here Are All The Major Crypto Firms Facing Charges From Regulators This Year. Retrieved from https://www.forbes.com/sites/tylerroush/2023/03/29/crypto-crackdown-here-are-all-the-major-crypto-firms-facing-charges-from-regulators-this-year/?sh=3f3b89eb4727

16. CoinDesk. (2023). CoinDesk Editorial: It Sure Looks Like The U.S. Is Trying To Kill Crypto. Retrieved from https://www.coindesk.com/consensus-magazine/2023/03/30/coindesk-editorial-it-sure-looks-like-the-us-is-trying-to-kill-crypto/

17. The Wall Street Journal. (n.d.). Decentralized Cryptocurrency Markets Threaten U.S. National Security, Treasury Says. Retrieved from https://www.wsj.com/articles/decentralized-cryptocurrency-markets-threaten-u-s-national-security-treasury-says-d9dd324f

18. Decrypt. (n.d.). SEC Out to Damage or Destroy Crypto Industry: LBRY CEO. Retrieved from https://decrypt.co/110468/sec-out-to-damage-or-destroy-crypto-industry-lbry-ceo

19. New Hampshire Business Review. (n.d.). Judge backs SEC in case against New Hampshire-based crypto firm. Retrieved from https://www.nhbr.com/judge-backs-sec-in-case-against-new-hampshire-based-crypto-firm/

20. Union Leader. (n.d.). LBRY founder decries precedent, likely to pay $50K in SEC case. Retrieved from https://www.unionleader.com/news/courts/lbry-founder-decries-precedent-likely-to-pay-50k-in-sec-case/article_5cf07001-5491-5d84-8d77-735849bc59c0.html

21. Yahoo News. (n.d.). SEC goes after Manchester startup for issuing cryptocurrency. Retrieved from https://news.yahoo.com/sec-goes-manchester-startup-issuing-080300114.html

22. The Information. (n.d.). The SEC v. LBRY: How a New Hampshire Court Battle Could Rewrite the Rules of Crypto. Retrieved from https://www.theinformation.com/articles/the-sec-v-lbry-how-a-new-hampshire-court-battle-could-rewrite-the-rules-of-crypto

23. ZyCrypto. (n.d.). LBRY's Jeremy Kauffman Says The SEC Is Out To Damage The Crypto Industry. Retrieved from https://zycrypto.com/lbrys-jeremy-kauffman-says-the-sec-is-out-to-damage-the-crypto-industry/

24. Concord Monitor. (n.d.). LBRY crypto token SEC securities legal nh new hampshire. Retrieved from https://www.concordmonitor.com/LBRY-crypto-token-SEC-securities-legal-nh-new-hampshire-39755562

25. Free Keene. (2022). Day 1 of the Crypto6 Trial: Ian's Lawyer Puts on a Strong Defense. Retrieved from

https://freekeene.com/2022/12/07/day-1-of-the-crypto6-trial-ians-lawyer-puts-on-a-strong-defense/

26. Forbes. (2023). Crypto Crackdown: Here Are All The Major Crypto Firms Facing Charges From Regulators This Year. Retrieved from https://www.forbes.com/sites/tylerroush/2023/03/29/crypto-crackdown-here-are-all-the-major-crypto-firms-facing-charges-from-regulators-this-year/?sh=3f3b89eb4727

27. CoinDesk. (2023). CoinDesk Editorial: It Sure Looks Like The U.S. Is Trying To Kill Crypto. Retrieved from https://www.coindesk.com/consensus-magazine/2023/03/30/coindesk-editorial-it-sure-looks-like-the-us-is-trying-to-kill-crypto/

28. The Wall Street Journal. (n.d.). Decentralized Cryptocurrency Markets Threaten U.S. National Security, Treasury Says. Retrieved from https://www.wsj.com/articles/decentralized-cryptocurrency-markets-threaten-u-s-national-security-treasury-says-d9dd324f

29. Decrypt. (n.d.). SEC Out to Damage or Destroy Crypto Industry: LBRY CEO. Retrieved from https://decrypt.co/110468/sec-out-to-damage-or-destroy-crypto-industry-lbry-ceo

30. New Hampshire Business Review. (n.d.). Judge backs SEC in case against New Hampshire-based crypto firm. Retrieved from https://www.nhbr.com/judge-backs-sec-in-case-against-new-hampshire-based-crypto-firm/

31. Union Leader. (n.d.). LBRY founder decries precedent, likely to pay $50K in SEC case. Retrieved from https://www.unionleader.com/news/courts/lbry-founder-decries-precedent-likely-to-pay-50k-in-

sec-case/article_5cf07001-5491-5d84-8d77-735849bc59c0.html
32. Yahoo News. (n.d.). SEC goes after Manchester startup for issuing cryptocurrency. Retrieved from https://news.yahoo.com/sec-goes-manchester-startup-issuing-080300114.html
33. The Information. (n.d.). The SEC v. LBRY: How a New Hampshire Court Battle Could Rewrite the Rules of Crypto. Retrieved from https://www.theinformation.com/articles/the-sec-v-lbry-how-a-new-hampshire-court-battle-could-rewrite-the-rules-of-crypto
34. ZyCrypto. (n.d.). LBRY's Jeremy Kauffman Says The SEC Is Out To Damage The Crypto Industry. Retrieved from https://zycrypto.com/lbrys-jeremy-kauffman-says-the-sec-is-out-to-damage-the-crypto-industry/
35. Concord Monitor. (n.d.). LBRY crypto token SEC securities legal nh new hampshire. Retrieved from https://www.concordmonitor.com/LBRY-crypto-token-SEC-securities-legal-nh-new-hampshire-39755562
36. Free Keene. (2022). Day 1 of the Crypto6 Trial: Ian's Lawyer Puts on a Strong Defense. Retrieved from https://freekeene.com/2022/12/07/day-1-of-the-crypto6-trial-ians-lawyer-puts-on-a-strong-defense/ CoinDesk. (n.d.). Is Bitcoin Legal? Retrieved from https://www.coindesk.com/learn/is-bitcoin-legal/
37. Fox Business. (n.d.). TikTok poses legitimate national security concerns: Treasury Secretary Yellen. Retrieved from https://www.foxbusiness.com/politics/tiktok-

poses-legitimate-national-security-concerns-treasury-secretary-yellen

38. Investor's Business Daily. (n.d.). Binance Accused of Money Laundering, Criminal Activity by Senators, Bitcoin Retreats. Retrieved from https://www.investors.com/news/binance-accused-of-money-laundering-criminal-activity-by-senators-bitcoin-retreats/

Chapter 7 References

1. Barsky, R. B., & Summers, L. H. (1988). Gibson's Paradox and the Gold Standard. Journal of Political Economy, 96(3), 528-550.
2. Eichengreen, B., & Flandreau, M. (2009). The rise and fall of the dollar (or when did the dollar replace sterling as the leading reserve currency?). European Review of Economic History, 13(3), 377-411.
3. Federal Reserve Bank of St. Louis. (2021). Consumer Price Index for All Urban Consumers. Retrieved from https://fred.stlouisfed.org/series/CPIAUCNS
4. Ferguson, N. (2008). The Ascent of Money: A Financial History of the World. New York: Penguin Press.
5. Friedman, M., & Schwartz, A. J. (1963). A Monetary History of the United States, 1867-1960. Princeton, NJ: Princeton University Press.
6. Griffin, G. E. (1994). The Creature from Jekyll Island: A Second Look at the Federal Reserve. Westlake Village, CA: American Media.
7. Icke, D. (1999). The Biggest Secret: The Book That Will Change the World. Scottsdale, AZ: Bridge of Love Publications.

8. Jastram, R. W. (1977). The Golden Constant: The English and American Experience 1560-1976. New York: Wiley.

9. Keynes, J. M. (1919). The Economic Consequences of the Peace. New York: Harcourt, Brace, and Howe.

10. Menger, K. (2002). The Monetary Stability of Gold. Journal of Institutional and Theoretical Economics, 158(4), 609-622.

11. Ritter, L. S., & Silber, W. L. (1989). The Story of Silver: How the White Metal Shaped America and the Modern World. Princeton, NJ: Princeton University Press.

12. U.S. Geological Survey. (2021). Mineral Commodity Summaries. Retrieved from https://pubs.usgs.gov/periodicals/mcs2021/mcs2021.pdf

13. U.S. Mint. (2021). American Eagle Gold Bullion Coins. Retrieved from https://www.usmint.gov/coins/coin-medal-programs/american-eagle-gold-bullion

14. World Gold Council. (2021). Gold Market Data and Statistics. Retrieved from https://www.gold.org/goldhub/data

15. Zweig, J. (2007). The Wall Street Journal Guide to Understanding Money and Investing. New York: Fireside.

16. MacLeod, A. (2018). Gold's Century: Manipulation and Geopolitics. GoldMoney Insights. Retrieved from https://www.goldmoney.com/research/goldmoney-insights/gold-s-century-manipulation-and-geopolitics

17. United States Government Accountability Office. (2011). Audit of the Department of the Treasury's Schedule of United States Gold Reserves Held by Federal Reserve Banks as of

September 30, 2010. Retrieved from
https://www.gao.gov/products/gao-11-768
18. Galbraith, J. K. (1975). Money: Whence It
Came, Where It Went. Boston: Houghton
Mifflin.
19. Witt, R. G. (1999). Gold, Prices and Wages
under the Greenback Standard. The Journal of
Economic History, 59(1), 216-218.
20. Clarke, S. V. (1967). Central Bank Cooperation
1924-31. Federal Reserve Bank of New York,
49(12), 1669-1696.
21. Yergin, D. (2006). The Prize: The Epic Quest for
Oil, Money & Power. New York: Free Press.
22. Chinn, M. D., & Frankel, J. A. (2007). Will the
Euro Eventually Surpass the Dollar as Leading
International Reserve Currency?. In G7 Current
Account Imbalances: Sustainability and
Adjustment (pp. 283-338). University of Chicago
Press.
23. Eichengreen, B. (2011). Exorbitant Privilege:
The Rise and Fall of the Dollar and the Future of
the International Monetary System. New York:
Oxford University Press.

Chapter 8 References

1. Maloney, M. (2015). Guide to Investing in Gold
and Silver: Protect Your Financial Future.
Business Plus.
2. Engelhard Corporation. (2012). The Engelhard
Silver Story. Retrieved from
https://www.silverinstitute.org/wp-
content/uploads/2015/09/Engelhard_Silver_Story
.pdf
3. World Silver Survey. (2021). World Silver
Survey 2021. The Silver Institute. Retrieved

from https://www.silverinstitute.org/wp-content/uploads/2021/04/WSS21.pdf

4. Smith, A. (2022). How to Invest in Silver. The Balance. Retrieved from https://www.thebalance.com/how-to-invest-in-silver-4172795

5. Berr, J. (2021). Why Silver Is a Popular Investment Right Now. Investopedia. Retrieved from https://www.investopedia.com/articles/investing/012916/why-silver-popular-investment-right-now.asp

6. Koos, J. (2021). The Case for Investing in Silver. U.S. News & World Report. Retrieved from https://money.usnews.com/investing/articles/the-case-for-investing-in-silver

7. McFarlin, M. (2020). Silver ETFs: The Ultimate Guide. ETF Database. Retrieved from https://etfdb.com/commodity/silver-etfs/

8. Zanoni, B. (2021). A Beginner's Guide to Investing in Silver. The Motley Fool. Retrieved from https://www.fool.com/investing/2021/07/31/a-beginners-guide-to-investing-in-silver/

9. Stovall, J. (2021). Investing in Precious Metals: Gold and Silver Stocks. Investopedia. Retrieved from https://www.investopedia.com/investing/investing-in-gold-and-silver-stocks/

10. Monex Precious Metals. (n.d.). Why Buy Silver? Monex. Retrieved from https://www.monex.com/why-buy-silver/

11. "The Great Silver Crime" by Theodore Butler, Silver Seek, January 21, 2021, https://silverseek.com/article/great-silver-crime-19084

12. "What Is Silver?" by American Elements, American Elements, https://www.americanelements.com/silver

13. "Silver Chemical Element - Reaction, Water, Uses, Elements, Metal, Gas, Number, Name, Symbol, Density, Silver" by Encyclopedia Britannica, Encyclopedia Britannica, https://www.britannica.com/science/silver-chemical-element

14. "Silver Supply/Demand Forecast: Increased Demand For Industrial Applications To Outpace Weaker Jewelry, Silverware Sales" by MetalMiner, January 11, 2021, https://agmetalminer.com/2021/01/11/silver-supply-demand-forecast-increased-demand-for-industrial-applications-to-outpace-weaker-jewelry-silverware-sales/

15. "What Is Silver Used For?" by The Silver Institute, The Silver Institute, https://www.silverinstitute.org/silver-uses/

16. "What is Self-Custody?" by Bitcoin Magazine, Bitcoin Magazine, March 2, 2021, https://bitcoinmagazine.com/guides/what-is-self-custody

17. "What is Hardware Wallet?" by Coindesk, Coindesk, https://www.coindesk.com/what-is-a-hardware-wallet

18. "Self-Custody" by Bitcoin Wiki, Bitcoin Wiki, March 5, 2021, https://en.bitcoin.it/wiki/Self-custody

19. "10 Best Silver IRA Companies of 2021" by Retirement Living, Retirement Living, https://www.retirementliving.com/best-silver-ira-companies

20. "The Five Best Places to Buy Silver in 2021" by The Balance, The Balance, March 18, 2021,

https://www.thebalance.com/best-places-to-buy-silver-4172693

21. "How to Buy Silver Coins & Bars" by Money Crashers, Money Crashers, March 22, 2021, https://www.moneycrashers.com/buy-silver-coins-bars-invest/

22. "The Silver Investor's Handbook: How to Invest in Silver and Minimize Risks" by Paul Mladjenovic, Wiley, 2012.

23. "The Big Silver Short: How a Reddit mob sent prices soaring" by Steve Goldstein, MarketWatch, February 1, 2021, https://www.marketwatch.com/story/the-big-silver-short-how-a-reddit-mob-sent-prices-soaring-11612151263

24. "WallStreetBets turns its attention to silver and mining stocks as Reddit-fueled surge continues" by Pippa Stevens, CNBC, February 1, 2021, https://www.cnbc.com/2021/02/01/wallstreetbets-turns-attention-to-silver-mining-stocks.html

25. "Warren Buffett: The World's Greatest Money Maker" by Robert G. Hagstrom, John Wiley & Sons, 2005.

26. "The Creature from Jekyll Island: A Second Look at the Federal Reserve" by G. Edward Griffin, American Media, 2010.

27. "The Biggest Secret: The Book That Will Change the World" by David Icke, Bridge of Love, 2010.

Chapter 9 References

1. Maloney, M. (2015). Guide to Investing in Gold and Silver: Protect Your Financial Future. Business Plus.

2. Engelhard Corporation. (2012). The Engelhard Silver Story. Retrieved from https://www.silverinstitute.org/wp-content/uploads/2015/09/Engelhard_Silver_Story.pdf

3. World Silver Survey. (2021). World Silver Survey 2021. The Silver Institute. Retrieved from https://www.silverinstitute.org/wp-content/uploads/2021/04/WSS21.pdf

4. Smith, A. (2022). How to Invest in Silver. The Balance. Retrieved from https://www.thebalance.com/how-to-invest-in-silver-4172795

5. Berr, J. (2021). Why Silver Is a Popular Investment Right Now. Investopedia. Retrieved from https://www.investopedia.com/articles/investing/012916/why-silver-popular-investment-right-now.asp

6. Koos, J. (2021). The Case for Investing in Silver. U.S. News & World Report. Retrieved from https://money.usnews.com/investing/articles/the-case-for-investing-in-silver

7. McFarlin, M. (2020). Silver ETFs: The Ultimate Guide. ETF Database. Retrieved from https://etfdb.com/commodity/silver-etfs/

8. Zanoni, B. (2021). A Beginner's Guide to Investing in Silver. The Motley Fool. Retrieved from https://www.fool.com/investing/2021/07/31/a-beginners-guide-to-investing-in-silver/

9. Stovall, J. (2021). Investing in Precious Metals: Gold and Silver Stocks. Investopedia. Retrieved from https://www.investopedia.com/investing/investing-in-gold-and-silver-stocks/

10. Monex Precious Metals. (n.d.). Why Buy Silver? Monex. Retrieved from https://www.monex.com/why-buy-silver/
11. "The Great Silver Crime" by Theodore Butler, Silver Seek, January 21, 2021, https://silverseek.com/article/great-silver-crime-19084
12. "What Is Silver?" by American Elements, American Elements, https://www.americanelements.com/silver
13. "Silver Chemical Element - Reaction, Water, Uses, Elements, Metal, Gas, Number, Name, Symbol, Density, Silver" by Encyclopedia Britannica, Encyclopedia Britannica, https://www.britannica.com/science/silver-chemical-element
14. "Silver Supply/Demand Forecast: Increased Demand For Industrial Applications To Outpace Weaker Jewelry, Silverware Sales" by MetalMiner, January 11, 2021, https://agmetalminer.com/2021/01/11/silver-supply-demand-forecast-increased-demand-for-industrial-applications-to-outpace-weaker-jewelry-silverware-sales/
15. "What Is Silver Used For?" by The Silver Institute, The Silver Institute, https://www.silverinstitute.org/silver-uses/
16. "What is Self-Custody?" by Bitcoin Magazine, Bitcoin Magazine, March 2, 2021, https://bitcoinmagazine.com/guides/what-is-self-custody
17. "What is Hardware Wallet?" by Coindesk, Coindesk, https://www.coindesk.com/what-is-a-hardware-wallet
18. "Self-Custody" by Bitcoin Wiki, Bitcoin Wiki, March 5, 2021, https://en.bitcoin.it/wiki/Self-custody

19. "10 Best Silver IRA Companies of 2021" by Retirement Living, Retirement Living, https://www.retirementliving.com/best-silver-ira-companies

20. "The Five Best Places to Buy Silver in 2021" by The Balance, The Balance, March 18, 2021, https://www.thebalance.com/best-places-to-buy-silver-4172693

21. "How to Buy Silver Coins & Bars" by Money Crashers, Money Crashers, March 22, 2021, https://www.moneycrashers.com/buy-silver-coins-bars-invest/

22. "The Silver Investor's Handbook: How to Invest in Silver and Minimize Risks" by Paul Mladjenovic, Wiley, 2012.

23. "The Big Silver Short: How a Reddit mob sent prices soaring" by Steve Goldstein, MarketWatch, February 1, 2021, https://www.marketwatch.com/story/the-big-silver-short-how-a-reddit-mob-sent-prices-soaring-11612151263

24. "WallStreetBets turns its attention to silver and mining stocks as Reddit-fueled surge continues" by Pippa Stevens, CNBC, February 1, 2021, https://www.cnbc.com/2021/02/01/wallstreetbets-turns-attention-to-silver-mining-stocks.html

25. "Warren Buffett: The World's Greatest Money Maker" by Robert G. Hagstrom, John Wiley & Sons, 2005.

26. "The Creature from Jekyll Island: A Second Look at the Federal Reserve" by G. Edward Griffin, American Media, 2010.

27. "The Biggest Secret: The Book That Will Change the World" by David Icke, Bridge of Love, 2010.

Made in the USA
Monee, IL
06 November 2023

45871059R00149